LET'S MAKE PIZZA!

For general information on our other products and services or to obtain technical support, please contact our Customer Care Department within the U.S. at (866) 744-2665, or outside the U.S. at (510) 253-0500.

Rockridge Press publishes its books in a variety of electronic and print formats. Some content that appears in print may not be available in electronic books, and vice versa.

TRADEMARKS: Rockridge Press and the Rockridge Press logo are trademarks or registered trademarks of Callisto Media Inc. and/or its affiliates, in the United States and other countries, and may not be used without written permission. All other trademarks are the property of their respective owners. Rockridge Press is not associated with any product or vendor mentioned in this book.

Front cover photography © Kelly Ishikawa; author photo © Grace Huang; Interior photography © Oliver Brachat/ Stockfood, p.3; Alessio Bogani/Stocksy, p.4; PhotoCuisine/ Thys/Supperdelux/Stockfood, p.6; Danil Nevsky/Stocksy, p.8; Tatjana Ristanic/Stocksy, p.17; Ellie Baygulov/Stocksy, p.21; Marc O. Finley/Stockfood, p.22; Daniel Aeschlimann/ Stockfood, p.38; Gräfe & Unzer Verlag/Julia Hoersch/ Stockfood, p.52; Don Crossland/Stockfood, p.54; Harald Walker/Stocksy, p.72; Jonathan Gregson/Stockfood, p.76; PhotoCuisine/Roulier/Turiot/Stockfood, p.98; Harald Walker/Stocksy, p.100; Great Stock!/Stockfood, p.134; Jan-Peter Westermann/Stockfood, p.136; Andrijana Kostova/Stocksy, p.156; Laura Adani/Stocksy, p.174

ISBN: Print 978-1-62315-732-6
eBook 978-1-62315-733-3

Let's Make
PIZZA!

A Pizza Cookbook to
Bring the Whole Family Together

Kathryn Kellinger

ROCKRIDGE
PRESS

CONTENTS

INTRODUCTION

Pizza night. It's one of the most crowd-pleasing events in the family meal hall of fame. Rare is the child who doesn't count pizza amongst their favorites, and rarer still is the parent who isn't grateful for a dinner that's fast, customizable, healthy, phenomenally delicious, and best of all, makes everyone happy.

For some, pizza is a speed-dial solution. For others it's a high-minded pursuit with investigations into flours, gluten levels, and meteoric oven temperatures. But for me, pizza is a chill-out family tradition—the time each week when we cook together, reconnect, and laugh it up. It's a touch-base built around basic but profound pleasures: having fun together and eating delicious food made exactly as we want it.

Pizza is often a kid's first foray into savory cooking, and, as a parent, I'm fascinated by watching them explore the imaginative, the adventurous, the safe and steady. Their personalities and their palates tend to be similar to my own. I've watched perfectionist five-year-olds arrange cherry tomatoes in diamond shapes and artistic seven-year-olds make self-portrait pizzas with red onion smiles, but more times than I can count, I've watched kids confidently shape dough and spread sauce and cheese to make themselves something delicious and satisfying. Pizza doesn't have to look neat or perfect, and kids find that liberating. They're natural-born pizza masters.

For parents, pizza night (or afternoon) offers us the freedom to tailor the toppings to suit our own tastes. While the little ones make their own edible masterpieces, parents do the same with next-level ingredients: clams and grilled summer corn, hand-made cured meats, or prosciutto with figs. Pizza night can be as simple or sophisticated as the maker, but what's especially unique is that this kid-friendly cuisine can coexist alongside a guest-worthy dinner, bringing everyone to the same table. Pizza is the only food I know of that offers this kind of universal culinary cohesion.

The recipes in this book are designed to be accessible to home cooks of all skill levels, adaptable to every type of eater (yes, even the gluten-frees and vegans!), and made with love, laughter, and good conversation. As kids grow, so do their tastes. That flexibility—that openness to trying new things—is one of the ways we gauge that they're growing up. One of the best things about pizza night is the mood that comes with it. Memories, along with dinner, are in the making.

IT'S PIZZA NIGHT!

Pizza making is interactive. From a cooking standpoint, that means it's tactile; you're handling and communicating with the ingredients. But for families cooking together, the interaction is face to face and in real time. Kids, with dough on their hands, drop the devices and live in the moment.

While parents might aim for a precise pizza circle topped by farmers' market finery, kids often have a different ideal in mind. Pizza might take the shape of a red-sauced Valentine or Mickey Mouse rendered in tomatoes and cheese. That both of these mindsets can exist side by side is one of the true joys of family pizza night.

Think of pizza night as a weekly touch-base, an opportunity to turn on the tunes and let family life take shape. Precious time together and a great meal? It's one of parenting's easiest win/wins.

How to Build a Perfect Pizza

THE INGREDIENTS

YEAST. Yeast is the living organism that animates dough. The recipes in this book use active dry yeast (not rapid rise or fresh yeast). Active dry yeast is sold in conjoined paper envelopes and can be found in the baking section of any chain supermarket. Combine the yeast with the indicated amount of water and set it aside, giving it 5 minutes or so to foam on the surface of the water. If it fails to bloom, the yeast is no longer active. Discard and start again with a fresh packet of yeast.

FLOUR. Have plenty on hand, and pizza will always be at your fingertips. While pizza purists insist on "OO" imported Italian flour, all-purpose flour makes a respectable crust and has the added benefit of being available everywhere. Bread flour makes for a sturdy dough, so if you have some on hand, experiment with combining bread flour with all-purpose, half and half.

SAUCE. Thinner than most pasta sauces, pizza sauce is meant to be spread. The homemade variety is a simple concoction of canned tomatoes simmered with salt, a little oregano, onions, garlic, and a pinch of sugar. It's the essence of simple, fast cooking, easily altered with red pepper flakes, herbs, or a hit of vinegar. Jarred sauce can offer a world of ready-to-eat variety, depth, and textures.

CHEESE. For most, only mozzarella cheese will do: Its meltability, signature stretch, and creamy but firm texture make it an integral part of the ideal pizza experience. The low moisture content of cow's milk mozzarella is key in achieving distinctly New York–style "mozz" qualities, while Neapolitan fans prefer the creamier mozzarella made from the milk of water buffaloes.

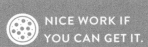

NICE WORK IF YOU CAN GET IT.
According to Seriouseats.com, the Italian pizza police, also known as Associazione Verace Pizza Napoletana (AVPN), guard and maintain the traditions of authentic Neapolitan pizza by upholding strict standards that require, among other criteria, bell-shaped ovens, hand-stretched doughs, wood fires, and cooking without pans.

NEED-TO-KNOW TIPS

PROPERLY PREHEAT. A hot oven is key for a good, crisp crust, and getting there takes time. Preheat the oven (and the pizza stone, if using) for at least 30 minutes or, better yet, 1 hour before you plan to bake your pizza.

ROLL IT OUT. A rolling pin moves the middle of the dough outward evenly and efficiently. Give the dough a few quick rolls followed by a quarter turn to the right, then repeat. This technique is great for kids who have difficulty with hand shaping. Always roll your dough out as thinly as possible.

MAKE MORE. The first rule of dough is to not overhandle it, but more often than not, kids just can't resist. Maximize the good times by encouraging experimentation and preparing for possible mistakes. Have a few extra balls of dough on hand so kids can poke, prod, and explore the dough without jeopardizing dinner.

A PRINTED PIE? *NASA scientists have developed a 3-D printer that makes pizza to feed astronauts on deep space missions. According to NASA's website, the machine creates a whole pie in 70 seconds, spraying on flavor, smell, and even micronutrients.*

EXERCISE RESTRAINT. It's easy to overload your pizza when faced with a smorgasbord of tasty toppings, but the crust—and your palate—can only handle so many. Max out at three toppings per pie so you can taste them all in harmony.

FIND THE PERFECT RATIO. Without getting into complicated math formulas, the goal is to taste a bit of everything in each bite. The toppings should be arranged in a single layer on top of the cheese with little to no overlap.

FINISH BIG. As soon as it comes out of the oven, give each pizza a drizzle of good-quality olive oil, a sprinkle of fresh, torn, or snipped herbs, and a few grinds of black pepper. The aroma alone will elevate your pizza game to pro status.

GIVE IT A REST. Wait a few minutes before slicing your fresh-baked pizza. This will allow the cheese to "set" and keep the toppings from slipping off the crust midbite.

Tools of the Trade

To make good pizza dough, all you really need are clean hands, a bowl, and a wooden spoon. That being said, there are certain home appliances and small professional tools that can make the process even easier. Here are the best options:

WHAT YOU NEED

FOOD PROCESSOR. Simply Amazing Pizza Dough (page 25) takes mere minutes in the work bowl of a food processor. A quick spin, followed by just a few minutes of hand kneading, results in a smooth, pliable dough every single time—bankable results.

KITCHENAID MIXER. Another dependable method of combining ingredients and effortlessly kneading them into a warm, yeasty dough. As with a food processor, a stand-up mixer, such as a KitchenAid, fitted with a dough hook blends and kneads dough efficiently with consistent results.

PIZZA PEEL. Shaped like a long-handled spatula with a whisper-thin front edge, a peel makes transporting pizza safe and easy: The dough can be rolled out and stretched on its broad surface, sauced and topped, then safely transported to the hot oven. A little practice in sliding the dough off the peel is all you'll need to gain pro-level expertise.

PIZZA STONE OR PIZZA STEEL. Made to mimic the heat-retaining ceramic floor of a wood-burning brick oven, a pizza stone or steel gets preheated along with the oven. On the heated stone, the dough crisps up beautifully. Pizza stones, heavy and often hot, can live permanently on the lower shelf of your oven. Use a peel or rimless baking sheet to get pies on and off the stone.

RIMLESS BAKING SHEET. In lieu of a pizza stone and peel, a rimless baking sheet is a useful tool in pizza making. It's more versatile than round rimmed pizza pans, as it does double duty as a cooking surface and a pizza peel, and the best part is that you probably already have it in your kitchen. Stretch and shape the dough on the baking sheet, cook the pizza on it, and then easily slide the piping-hot pizza onto a wooden cutting board for slicing and serving. Bonus points if you have two, allowing for two pizzas to cook at the same time.

WHEEL SLICER. In the same way a great ice cream scoop feels good in the hand and makes the job easier, a wheel slicer elevates the pizza experience.

BENCH SCRAPER. This magnificent, inexpensive professional tool helps in both lifting sticky dough and scraping floured surfaces clean. It also acts as a knife to divide balls of dough into two or four pieces.

SKIP IT

COUNTERTOP PLUG-IN PIZZA OVENS. Though they promise higher temperatures than regular ovens can deliver, many of these countertop clunkers are needlessly expensive. Conserve your cash and counter space: Your home oven is just fine.

BREAD MACHINES. Food processors and standing mixers both put out admirable pizza dough and are multitasking workhorses. The most efficient kitchens avoid one-trick ponies.

NON-CONTACT THERMOMETERS. Hand-held infrared thermometers are the domain of die-hard pizza geeks with backyard brick ovens, not of us regular home cooks. If you want to determine whether your oven calibration is high, low, or right on target, a simple (and much cheaper) hanging oven thermometer from the hardware store will do the trick.

FRIDAY NIGHT PIZZA. *According to the Paul Moses book An Unlikely Union, in the early 1900s, Italians in America adopted the ritual of Friday night pizza, which allowed for the Catholic practice of abstaining from meat on Fridays. This tradition continued with other pizza-loving Catholics throughout the country, and today, half of all pizza purchased in the United States is sold on Friday and Saturday nights.*

GET GRILLING

The best reason to grill pizza? It keeps the heat outside. The other best reason to grill pizza? The love! It's been my long-established rule that all summer entertaining (except for pig roasts) revolve around grilled pizza. The doughs are made in advance, allowing my husband and me to hang with our guests and then gather round as a group to make our own pizza. The morning shopping trip is a fun part of it, too: We write a quick list and then head to the farmers' market to gather toppings, letting fresh ingredients spark our pizza inspiration. Much of our summer social life is built around grilling pizza. It's one of our favorite ways to celebrate the many joys of the most outdoor season.

Plan on a couple of practice sessions to understand the relationship between fire and dough. There's a learning curve to grilling pizza, which can be a rewarding part of a pizza journey. Plus, you can eat your mistakes.

Refrigerate prepared dough (Simply Amazing Pizza Dough, page 25; Pro Dough, page 27; or Italian-Herbed Pizza Dough, page 37) on a parchment-lined baking sheet, and bring it out to the grill just before cooking.

1. Preheat an outdoor grill, either charcoal or propane, for at least 1 hour before you're ready to cook your pizza. The goal is high but indirect heat. Position the coals to one side, using a chimney starter to replenish the coals if necessary. If you're using a propane grill, turn one of the burners to high and leave the other burner turned off. Keep the lid closed—the hotter the grill, the lower the chances of pizza dough sticking to the grates.

2. Have everything at your fingertips. Place a table next to the grill set with a wooden cutting board and rolling pin, sauce, cheese, toppings, olive oil, salt, pepper, seasonings, a pastry brush, a spatula, and tongs.

3. Stretch and shape the dough, brush the surface with olive oil, and place the dough oil-side down on the grill near, but not directly over, the heat source.

4. Grill the dough for about 3 minutes (adjust the dough's position as needed for more or less heat), then brush the top side with oil and flip it over. Top the crust with sauce, cheese, and toppings, close the grill's lid, and cook the pizza for 4 to 6 minutes, until the cheese has melted. Using a peel, carefully transfer the pizza to a cutting board; cool for 2 minutes, then slice and serve.

If kids are helping, transfer the crust to a cutting board after cooking both sides, let them help scatter on the toppings, and return the pizza to the grill to finish cooking.

Pizza Night Prep

Whether you're making two pies or ten, organization is the cornerstone of homemade pizza heaven.

There are those who like to chop, grate, and cook every component ahead of time and those who put it all together on the spot. But no matter what your personal pizza-making style may be, a little planning is always a solid move. Whenever I make pizza with my family, I leave a few prep tasks undone so that we can do them together. Salad spinning, cheese slicing and grating, and sautéing onions help kids develop kitchen skills, and doing these things together as a family helps kids develop something much more important—conversation skills.

THE NIGHT BEFORE

MAKE THE DOUGH. Let the dough rise overnight in the refrigerator, or transfer a batch of frozen dough to the refrigerator.

TAKE INVENTORY. Make use of any leftovers—spinach, cherry tomatoes, or even leftover rotisserie chicken and roasted vegetables—by building a pizza around them. Use the ingredients you already have on hand as a starting point, and write a list of extras you'll need to get at the store.

PREP YOUR MEAT. Pepperoni can be sliced ahead, and pancetta, bacon, or sausage can be browned the night before and refrigerated in separate airtight containers.

CRUMBLE SOFT CHEESES. If you're using feta, Gorgonzola, or goat cheese, crumble it the night before and refrigerate in separate airtight containers.

WASH, CHOP, AND/OR COOK VEGETABLES. Break broccoli down into florets, slice onions, blanch broccoli rabe, and refrigerate the prepped ingredients in separate airtight containers.

ON PIZZA NIGHT

PREHEAT. Take the dough out of the refrigerator and let it come to room temperature for about 40 minutes before using, while your oven preheats.

SLICE OR SHRED HARDER CHEESES. Soft cheeses can be crumbled the night before, but harder cheeses will dry out if prepped too far in advance.

CLEAN YOUR GREENS. Rinse and spin-dry all lettuces, herbs, and other greens so they'll be ready to top your pizza or be tossed into salad.

SET UP A PIZZA STATION. Clear off a dedicated area near the oven where everyone will form and top their pizzas. Group bowls of toppings on trays according to pizza type, and label them with sticky notes. This doesn't mean that pizza makers can't mix and match, but for those who don't want to think too much about it, the "recipe" is clear.

SET THE TABLE. Make it casual with stacks of plates, glasses, napkins, salad bowls, and beverages. It's a serve-yourself vibe that encourages everyone to mill around the kitchen or sit down and share slices.

ANY OLD TIME

PICK A PLAYLIST. You will need tunes. Think about asking everyone to contribute to a themed Pizza Night playlist. It's a great way to share older music and hear the new hits.

GET SAUCED. New York–Style Pizza Sauce (page 40) is a freezer staple to keep on hand. Make a double or triple recipe, portion it into separate resealable freezer bags, and store it in the freezer for up to 6 months. Thaw the sauce overnight in the refrigerator or in the microwave on pizza night.

CREATE YOUR CONDIMENTS. Having the sauce and dough ready to go can make pizza night extra easy, and the same holds true for condiments, such as Quick-Pickled Red Onions (page 47) or Black Olive Tapenade (page 45).

TASTE THIS!

Less is more when it comes to the number of toppings on a pizza, but the number of combinations is surely infinite. The art of free-form pizza making can span the globe or simply dig deep into the refrigerator.

Balance is the rule when blending textures and flavors: Pair a salty ingredient like olives with a creamy cheese like ricotta. Layer the natural sweetness of figs or other fruits with the sharp saltiness of a cured meat.

Begin with your main flavor ingredient and build a complete pizza around it. These are a few of my family's favorites:

- ▽ Sliced heirloom tomatoes over ricotta, drizzled with basil-infused oil
- ▽ Hot peppers and onions with sweet Italian sausage and mozzarella
- ▽ Grilled radicchio, diced pancetta, and ricotta
- ▽ Sautéed fennel, chopped herbs, and fresh goat cheese
- ▽ Balsamic-roasted garlic with butternut squash, arugula, and goat cheese
- ▽ Sun-dried tomatoes, endive, and Taleggio cheese
- ▽ Fire-roasted red peppers and smoked mozzarella cheese

- ▽ Autumn vegetables and Asiago cheese
- ▽ Grilled shrimp and pesto
- ▽ Clam and summer corn, drizzled with chili oil
- ▽ Escarole, red onion, and chopped walnuts with mozzarella and Parmesan cheeses

Experiment with different ingredients and take inspiration from the season to come up with your own perfect flavor partners.

Make It Your Own!

Pizza is endlessly customizable and offers the opportunity to have exactly the meal you want. So don't be shy—embrace the freedom and get creative as a family.

To ensure that there's enough pizza to go around, each dough recipe in this book will make two 12- to 14-inch pizzas. To make four personal pizzas instead, simply use a quarter of the sauce, cheese, and toppings on each instead of the half called for in the recipes. Divide the prepared dough as desired and shape it into balls (YouTube offers a veritable video encyclopedia on kneading and shaping pizza dough). Once it is shaped into a ball or balls, the dough can be frozen or refrigerated. Each recipe lists a recommended dough, but they can easily be swapped with whichever dough becomes your favorite.

For vegans and meat eaters, pizza is a rare common ground. There's room on any veggie pizza for vegan mozzarella, and you can serve diced browned pancetta, pepperoni, or other meaty accompaniments on the side for those who'd like to add them.

And then there're the kids. There are, in my world of families, all kinds of eaters. Some can correctly identify a maitake mushroom at ten paces while others remain deeply challenging to feed. One little girl will only eat grilled crust topped with olive oil and pink Hawaiian salt. The other kids once insisted to her that pizza requires cheese and sauce in order to actually be pizza. They now all know that Roman pizza bianca, with nothing but olive oil and salt, is considered one of the most elementally delicious of all pizzas. But it's always my hope that for the pickiest of eaters, there might be basil and, down the road, that could lead to other greens like spinach.

LONG DISTANCE DELIVERY. *According to the BBC, in 2001, Pizza Hut delivered a six-inch salami pizza to the International Space Station—the first pizza delivered to outer space. In a break with usual delivery practices, the Russian astronaut receiving the pie didn't have to pay for it. Instead, Pizza Hut paid about $1 million for the promotional privilege of being the first to deliver where no man had delivered before.*

While the kids enjoy their creations, grown-ups have the opportunity for adventurous eating: Use garlic scapes (the garlic's flower bud) to enliven a Prosciutto Cotto Pizza with Pesto & Spring Garlic (page 86); add pickled jalapeño to a Hawaiian Pizza (page 62); or save and chop the fennel fronds when preparing Fennel & Fontina Pizza with Olive Tapenade (page 45) and dust your pizza with the aromatic feathery greens. Throughout the book, you'll find tips such as "Adventurous addition" and "Keep it simple" to help create your perfect pie.

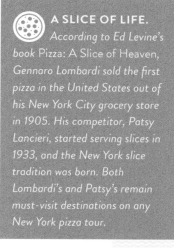

A SLICE OF LIFE. *According to Ed Levine's book* Pizza: A Slice of Heaven, *Gennaro Lombardi sold the first pizza in the United States out of his New York City grocery store in 1905. His competitor, Patsy Lancieri, started serving slices in 1933, and the New York slice tradition was born. Both Lombardi's and Patsy's remain must-visit destinations on any New York pizza tour.*

STORE-BOUGHT SAVIORS

Pizza night is a judgment-free zone. If a store-bought savior can help get dinner on the table—go for it! Any or all of the components of pizza making are available at the supermarket. The most important ingredient of pizza night is family fun. Grab what's needed on the way home. The brands that follow are widely available, offer a good flavor-to-value ratio, and have stood the test of side-by-side taste tests. They're reliable, tasty stand-ins for homemade pizza staples.

SAUCE

PREGO TRADITIONAL MARINARA. Available everywhere, this sauce has an especially bright tomato flavor and is a taste-test favorite.

BARILLA TRADITIONAL MARINARA. A chunkier sauce with good garlic flavor, this has good presence on the pie.

365 CLASSIC PASTA SAUCE. Whole Foods' house brand is tasty and organic.

DOUGH

USE YOUR NEIGHBORHOOD PIZZA SHOP AS A RESOURCE; they're usually happy to sell their sturdy, supple pizza dough. It's freshly made and a joy to work with.

WHOLE FOODS FRESH PACK PIZZA DOUGH. A silky dough that's easy to work with, it bakes nicely into a slightly softer, bread-like crust.

TRADER JOE'S TRADITIONAL and **GARLIC AND HERB PIZZA DOUGH.** Oiled hands and a well-floured surface will help you handle these stickier doughs. Both bake up into delicious, crispy, chewy crusts.

PILLSBURY WHOLE PIZZA DOUGH (whole-wheat and white flour). The advantage? It's available everywhere, and children are universally fascinated by dough in a tube.

BOB'S RED MILL NATURAL FOODS GLUTEN-FREE PIZZA CRUST MIX. Containing a blend of whole-grain rice and millet flours, this dough is easy to make and gets high marks for flavor and texture.

WHOLLY GLUTEN-FREE FROZEN PIZZA DOUGH. This ready-to-bake dough couldn't be more convenient for those on a gluten-free diet.

CHEESE

POLLY-O WHOLE MILK MOZZARELLA. The cheese of choice for New York pizzerias is widely available, has low moisture content, and offers the trademark mozz stretch that pizza eaters crave. Different from balls of fresh-made mozzarella, this is the cheese to use for Parlor Classics (page 55).

TRADER JOE'S FULL-FAT MOZZARELLA. With a good stretch and salty flavor, this mozzarella holds up well under the heat.

SORRENTO WHOLE MILK MOZZARELLA. A solid choice for flavor and meltability.

DAIYA VEGAN MOZZARELLA. One of the best parts of any pizza is the melted cheese. Melty, stretchy, and delicious with any combination of toppings, this vegan mozzarella does the job.

KITE HILL FRESH ALMOND MILK CHEESE. An artisanal nut-based cheese that employs the bacterial cultures and techniques used in dairy cheeses, Kite Hill has a very good complex flavor and crumbly texture.

FIELD ROAST CHAO CHEESE. Handmade, small-batch tofu cheeses flavored with garlic, cayenne, and tomato, silky, meltable Chao Cheese gets the "pizza worthy" award from dedicated vegans.

THE DOUGH

There is no one perfect dough: there are many, each with its own distinct strengths. Some bake up extra crisp, some have tangy flavor, and some create pizzas that are perfectly smooth while others are airier, with giant bubbles that puff up in the oven. Whether you're seeking a quick-rise recipe for weeknights or an artisanal-style dough that requires a bit of attention, in this chapter you'll find just the thing to fit your family's routine and pizza-night style.

Making pizza at home is a surprisingly easy process—one that gets simpler (and more addictive) with practice. Begin by choosing a dough that suits your current needs, and then, once you master one recipe, branch out and try the others. Some of these recipes can be made ahead and refrigerated or frozen for ultimate convenience. Whenever possible, I have included these instructions and other tips and tricks to help make pizza night a fun and rewarding experience for all.

FROM COUNTERTOP TO PIZZA STONE: A HOW-TO

The easiest way to transport a just-topped round of pizza dough onto a blazing hot pizza stone is by using a pizza peel. Just dust the peel with cornmeal or a little flour, then stretch the dough and place it on the broad surface of the peel before topping. Using quick little jerking motions, nudge the topped pizza from the peel to the hot stone in the oven. Once the pizza is done cooking, the peel, ever useful, then acts as a large-scale spatula, ideal for transferring the crispy pie to a board for cutting.

If you're using a pizza stone but don't have a peel, another great option is to use a rimless baking sheet to transport the topped dough to the oven. As they're aluminum, and somewhat stickier than the thin, smooth wood of a pizza peel, you might need a little more cornmeal or flour to help the pizza slide smoothly from baking sheet to pizza stone. If you don't have a rimless baking sheet, turn a standard baking sheet over and use it in the same way. To remove the hot pizza from the oven, use tongs or a spatula to gently lift and slide it back onto the baking sheet.

When making personal-size pizzas, stretching the dough and topping it on 12-inch squares of parchment paper can make the trip to the oven a simple one. The parchment paper can be used to transport the pizza by lifting it by the sides and then sliding the pizza onto the stone, or it can just be set directly on the stone along with the pizza. This method can work with larger pizzas, but it requires a degree more steadiness.

Whichever method you use, remember:

▼ Always open the oven and pull the oven rack and pizza stone out halfway before lifting your pizza from the kitchen counter—it's just plain safer than trying to do it with an uncooked pizza in your hand.

▼ If the dough overheats or is over-handled during the assembly process, it becomes stickier. Refrigerate it briefly (about 10 minutes), and it will become less "grabby." A quick cooling-off period will make it more cooperative, able to slide smoothly and cohesively into the oven.

Simply Amazing Pizza Dough

MAKES 2 (12- TO 14-INCH) PIZZAS OR 4 PERSONAL PIZZAS

This is a pizza dough miracle that can easily be committed to memory and whipped up anytime, anywhere. Sturdy and reliable, this dough offers choice; it can be made and used about an hour and a half later, or made in advance to be refrigerated or frozen.

Made in a food processor or standing mixer, the dough comes together in mere minutes. The smooth and supple dough is then kneaded by hand and divided into 2 or 4 pieces.

If making the dough in advance and freezing, batches should be mixed individually rather than doubled; doubling the recipe produces a dough too big for most machines. Just scrape the work bowl and shake out the excess flour and bits of dough between batches: Washing isn't necessary.

▼ NUT-FREE

▼ VEGAN

PREP TIME: 15 minutes
RISE TIME: 45 minutes
COOK TIME: None

1 package active dry yeast
1½ cups warm water (about 110° F)
2 tablespoons extra-virgin olive oil
4 cups all-purpose flour, plus more for dusting
1½ teaspoons salt

1 In a medium bowl, add the yeast to the warm water and let bloom for about 10 minutes. Add the olive oil.

2 In a food processor or standing mixer fitted with a paddle attachment, pulse to blend the flour and salt. With the machine running, add the yeast mixture in a slow, steady stream, mixing just until the dough comes together. Turn the dough out onto a well-floured board, and with lightly floured hands, knead the dough using the heels of your hands, pushing the dough and then folding it over. Shape it into a ball, then cut it into 2 or 4 equal pieces. ➤

3 Place the balls of dough on a lightly floured baking sheet and cover with a clean dishtowel. Let them rise in a warm, draft-free spot until they are doubled in size, about 45 minutes.

4 Proceed with the desired recipe.

TO USE LATER: *Before step 3, place the balls of dough on a parchment-lined baking sheet and cover with plastic wrap. Be sure to space the dough balls with room to expand, as they will double in size. Refrigerate for up to 24 hours. Remove from the refrigerator about 15 minutes before using.*

TO FREEZE: *Before step 3, dust each ball of dough with flour and place in individual resealable freezer bags. Store in the freezer for up to 1 month. To use, transfer the dough to the refrigerator the night before using it. The dough can also be used directly from the freezer by letting it come to room temperature for about 2 hours.*

Cooking with kids: *Challenge the kids to measure and organize ingredients on a sheet tray next to the food processor. An organized approach is the key to success even with the simplest recipes. (And the good news? Cooking is a recommended way of improving executive function skills in children; it's a win/win.)*

Pro Dough

MAKES 2 (12- TO 14-INCH) PIZZAS OR 4 PERSONAL PIZZAS

For those who want to deepen their pizza practice, this light, crisp Neapolitan-style crust bubbles with a strongly developed structure. With very little yeast, the dough requires two long (overnight) rises in the refrigerator to reach its fullest expression. With this dough, you can glimpse the difference in taste and texture between a fast rise and a lengthier one. The reward is an impressively tender, billowy, flavorful thin-crust pizza.

PREP TIME: 40 minutes
RISE TIME: 6 hours, plus overnight
COOK TIME: None

¼ teaspoon active dry yeast

1½ cups warm water

4 cups "00" flour or all-purpose flour, plus more for dusting

2 teaspoons salt

Extra-virgin olive oil, for greasing

1 In a medium bowl, add the yeast to the warm water and let it stand for 10 minutes. While the yeast is blooming, rinse the bowl of a standing mixer with hot water and dry thoroughly. It should be warm to the touch. In the warm mixing bowl, combine the flour and salt. Add the yeast mixture and mix on low speed with a dough hook for 2 minutes. Raise the speed to medium-low and continue to mix for about 10 minutes, until the dough is cohesive and smooth and has pulled away from the sides of the bowl.

2 Knead again on medium-low speed for an additional 10 minutes, or until the dough is soft and warm to the touch.

3 Transfer the dough to a large, lightly oiled bowl, rolling the dough to coat it on all sides. Cover with plastic wrap and refrigerate overnight.

4 The next day, transfer the dough to a lightly floured board and punch it down. Cut it into 2 or 4 equal pieces and shape into smooth balls. Lightly flour the balls, place them on a baking tray, and cover with a damp kitchen towel. Let the dough rise again in the refrigerator for at least 4 hours or overnight. ➤

5 Remove the dough from the refrigerator, place on a lightly floured baking sheet, and cover with a damp kitchen towel. Let it rise for 1½ to 2 hours, until it is doubled in size.

6 Proceed with the desired recipe.

A CLOSER LOOK: *"00" or double zero flour is fine-milled, low-protein flour that results in more delicate strands of gluten that take longer to build. Pizza purists insist on it for tender crusts.*

Whole-Wheat Pizza Dough

MAKES 2 (12- TO 14-INCH) PIZZAS OR 4 PERSONAL PIZZAS

Whole-wheat flour is an easy way to boost the health benefits of freshly made pizza. With a more pronounced flavor than white flour and a little more texture, it does well with stronger ingredients like roasted vegetables, and deeply flavored greens like broccoli rabe. Seek out King Arthur's Whole-Wheat Flour and its true, full wheat flavor.

▼
DAIRY-FREE
▼
NUT-FREE
▼
VEGETARIAN

PREP TIME: 15 minutes
RISE TIME: 1 hour
COOK TIME: None

2 cups warm water (110° F)

1 packet active dry yeast (2¼ teaspoons)

2 teaspoons sugar

4½ cups whole-wheat flour, divided, plus more for dusting

3 teaspoons salt

2 tablespoons extra-virgin olive oil

2 tablespoons honey

1 In the bowl of a standing mixer fitted with a dough hook, stir together the water, yeast, and sugar. Let it stand for 10 minutes.

2 Turn the mixer on low, and slowly add 2¼ cups of flour and the salt, olive oil, and honey. When all the ingredients are combined, add the remaining 2¼ cups of flour, and raise the speed to medium. Mix for 3 minutes, until the dough has come together.

3 Turn the dough out onto a well-floured board. Knead, using the heels of your hands, pressing the dough away and then folding it over itself. Repeat several times, then divide the dough into 2 or 4 equal pieces. Shape into balls and place on a parchment-lined baking sheet. Cover with a clean kitchen towel and let them rise until nearly doubled in volume, 30 minutes to 1 hour.

4 Proceed with the desired recipe.

COOKING TIP: *Whole-Wheat Pizza Dough takes longer to bake than one made with white flour (about 18 minutes at 450°F and 15 minutes at 500°F). If using a cheese that melts more quickly and browns (like mozzarella or vegan cheese), add it halfway through the baking process.*

Gluten-Free Pizza Dough

MAKES 1 (12- TO 14-INCH) PIZZA

Many gluten-free pizza dough recipes require multiple flours and stabilizing gums. This gluten-free dough, containing rice flour and the humble but flavorful potato, is closer in spirit to the simplicity of pizza. Approachable as well as tasty, the dough is easy to work with. Along with a little tapioca, the starch of the Idaho potato is what holds it all together, so be sure to seek it out specifically.

▼
DAIRY-FREE
▼
GLUTEN-FREE
▼
NUT-FREE
▼
VEGETARIAN

PREP TIME: 20 minutes
RISE TIME: 1½ hours
COOK TIME: 25 minutes

2 large Idaho potatoes
1 cup warm water
2 teaspoons honey
1 package active dry yeast
1 cup rice flour
½ cup tapioca starch
2 teaspoons salt
1 egg white
1 tablespoon extra-virgin olive oil

1 In a medium saucepan over medium-high heat, cover the washed and unpeeled potatoes with water and cook for 20 to 25 minutes, until easily pierced with a knife. Drain, cool, and remove the skin. Pass the potatoes through a ricer or grate using the large holes of a box grater.

2 In a medium bowl, stir together the warm water, honey, and yeast, and set aside for 5 minutes, until the yeast foams (if this doesn't happen, discard and begin again with new yeast).

3 In the bowl of a standing mixer fitted with the paddle attachment, combine the potatoes, rice flour, tapioca starch, and salt. Mix on medium speed until the mixture forms a coarse meal. (Before adding the wet ingredients, use a bit of this mixture to lightly flour a surface for use in step 5.) Add the egg white and oil, then add the yeast mixture in a slow, steady stream. Continue mixing until the dough comes together.

4 Cover the bowl with plastic wrap, and set aside until the dough rises by half, 1 to 1½ hours.

5 Turn the dough out onto a lightly floured surface and divide it into 2 or 4 pieces; shape each piece into a ball. Roll out and proceed with the desired recipe.

TO USE LATER: *Store each ball of dough individually in a resealable bag. Refrigerate for up to 24 hours.*

TO FREEZE: *Store each ball of dough individually in a resealable freezer bag, and freeze for up to 1 month.*

Cooking with kids: *Separating eggs is a fascinating process. With a bowl underneath, have the kids flip the yolk from shell to shell while the white drips and spills to the bowl below. The retained egg white gets added to the dough.*

No-Knead Pan Pizza Dough

MAKES 2 (13-BY-18-INCH) PIZZAS

This dough is a spin on the revolutionary kneading-free technique developed by New York baker Jim Lahey. It's as simple as mixing the dough and covering it with a towel; the most important ingredient is time. Left out at room temperature to rise for up to 18 hours, it develops into a delicious, bubbly crust. Made to fit into rectangular pans, this crust is a convenient choice for feeding a crowd. Not only is it one of the easiest doughs to master, it's one of the tastiest.

PREP TIME: 5 minutes, plus 30 minutes to rest
RISE TIME: 8 to 18 hours
COOK TIME: None

3½ cups bread flour, plus more for dusting
¼ teaspoon active dry yeast
1 teaspoon kosher salt
¾ teaspoon sugar
1⅓ cups warm water
Extra-virgin olive oil, for drizzling

1 In the bowl of a standing mixer fitted with the paddle attachment, combine the flour, yeast, salt, and sugar. With the mixer on low, add the water and mix just until combined, about 3 minutes.

2 Cover the bowl with a towel and let the mixture rise at room temperature for 8 to 18 hours, or until it is doubled in volume.

3 Turn the dough onto a well-floured board and divide in half. Lightly drizzle two large (13-by-18-inch) sheet pans with olive oil, and spread to cover with a thin, even coating.

4 Stretch one piece of dough to the length of the pan, then place it in the center of one pan. Gently pull and stretch the dough to fit the width. If it resists, refrigerate the dough for 10 minutes. When the dough fits the pan, cover the pan with a damp kitchen towel and let it rest for 30 minutes at room temperature. Repeat with the second piece of dough and the second sheet pan.

5 Proceed with the desired recipe.

 Cooking with kids: *This is practically a science experiment. But remember, no squeezing or poking the dough while it's rising!*

Cauliflower Pizza Dough

MAKES 1 (12- TO 14-INCH) PIZZA

This is a truly surprising and tasty answer to the gluten-free question. With no flour at all, think of this pizza crust as a large Parmesan crisp bulked up by cauliflower. Cauliflower, one of the world's most magical vegetables, is a chameleon: meaty when roasted, snappy when pickled, and here, the backbone of this ingenious trick toward cutting back on simple carbohydrates. Even in you don't live a gluten-free lifestyle, this is a fun twist on pizza.

PREP TIME: 15 minutes
RISE TIME: None
COOK TIME: 30 minutes

1 head cauliflower, cut into florets
½ cup shredded mozzarella or Mexican-blend cheese
¼ cup grated Parmesan cheese
½ teaspoon dried oregano
¼ teaspoon salt
¼ teaspoon garlic powder
2 eggs, lightly beaten

1 Preheat the oven to 400°F, and prepare a vegetable steamer.

2 Steam the cauliflower until fork tender, 6 to 8 minutes. When cool enough to handle, press the florets with paper towels to dry and remove as much moisture as possible.

3 Transfer the florets to a food processor and pulse just until the cauliflower resembles cooked rice, being careful not to let it liquefy.

4 Transfer the cauliflower "rice" to a large mixing bowl. (The cauliflower should be as dry as possible, so it might be necessary to press it again with paper towels.) Add the mozzarella, Parmesan, oregano, salt, garlic powder, and eggs. Stir well until fully combined and then transfer the mixture to a baking sheet. Spread the dough evenly into a circle and bake, untopped, for 20 minutes.

5 Remove the pizza crust from the oven, add toppings, and proceed with the desired recipe.

COOKING TIP: *Success with this gluten-free crust is dependent upon reducing the moisture in the cooked cauliflower. Also, a low-moisture packaged mozzarella, rather than fresh, works best.*

Focaccia

MAKES 1 (13-BY-18-INCH) FOCACCIA

Focaccia, a flatbread, is closely related to pizza but has a lighter, airier quality. It lends itself perfectly to savory fruits and herbs, simple vegetables, or no-bake pizzas when summer tomatoes are available in their glory. In addition to pizzas, Italian tuna with Peperonata (page 50) and lemon zest pressed between two small squares of focaccia is indeed sandwich heaven.

PREP TIME: 10 minutes, plus 1 hour to rest
RISE TIME: 3 hours
COOK TIME: 50 minutes

1 cup peeled and diced Yukon gold potatoes
  (2 medium potatoes)
4½ cups bread flour
1 packet active dry yeast
1 teaspoon sugar
1½ teaspoons kosher salt, divided
Extra-virgin olive oil, for greasing and drizzling

1 In a medium saucepan over high heat, cover the potatoes with cold water. Bring to a boil and cook until the potatoes are easily pierced with a fork, about 10 minutes. Ladle 1 cup of the cooking water into a blender, then drain the potatoes well. Put the drained potatoes in the blender with the cooking liquid, and purée. Set the potato purée aside to cool slightly.

2 In the bowl of a standing mixer fitted with the paddle attachment, combine the flour, yeast, sugar, and 1 teaspoon of salt. Add the potato purée and mix on low until a sticky dough forms. Cover the bowl with a towel and let it sit in a warm place until the dough has tripled in volume, 2 to 3 hours.

3 Lightly oil a large (13-by-18-inch) rimmed baking sheet. Use a rubber spatula to scrape the dough out onto the baking sheet. Pull the dough into the shape of the baking sheet and, with lightly oiled hands, use your fingertips to continue to press, spread, and dimple the dough. Try to create a uniform thickness as the dough spreads toward the rim of the pan.

4 Cover the dough with a clean dish towel and let it rest at room temperature for 1 hour. Halfway through the resting time, position the oven rack in the center of the oven and preheat to 400°F.

5 Drizzle with olive oil and sprinkle with the remaining ½ teaspoon of salt. Bake the focaccia for 30 to 40 minutes, until the top is evenly golden, turning the pan halfway through the cooking time.

Cooking with kids: *The surface of focaccia has a trademark "blistered" appearance, which is achieved by pressing your fingers into the dough like you're playing piano. This is the perfect task for kids, as their little fingers will create ideal dimples all over the dough.*

Deep-Dish Pizza Dough

MAKES 2 (12- TO 14-INCH) PIZZAS

Closer to a pie than Italian-style pizza, Chicago's skillet-style pizza is more of a pizza casserole. Deep-dish pizzas can travel—make it and take it—making them perfect for potlucks. Use one crust today and freeze the other.

▼

NUT-FREE

▼

VEGAN

PREP TIME: 15 minutes
RISE TIME: 1½ hours
COOK TIME: None

1 packet active dry yeast
1½ cups warm water
1 teaspoon sugar
3½ cups all-purpose flour, divided, plus more for dusting
½ cup cornmeal
1 teaspoon salt
½ cup extra-virgin olive oil plus 2 tablespoons, divided

1 In the bowl of a standing mixer fitted with a dough hook, stir together the yeast, water, and sugar. Let it stand for 5 minutes, until the mixture is foamy.

2 With the mixer on low, add 1½ cups of flour and the cornmeal, salt, and ½ cup of olive oil. Blend until the ingredients are smoothly incorporated.

3 Add the remaining 2 cups of flour, a quarter-cup at a time, until all is incorporated to form a sticky dough. Continue kneading for 3 to 5 minutes, until a smooth dough forms.

4 Turn the dough out onto a lightly floured surface, and divide into 2 equal pieces. Shape each piece into a ball.

5 Lightly coat a large bowl with the remaining 2 tablespoons of oil. Place the dough in the bowl, turn it to oil on all sides, and let it rise in a warm place until almost doubled, 1 to 1½ hours.

TO USE LATER: *Before step 5, place the balls of dough in individual resealable bags and refrigerator to rise overnight. Stand at room temperature for 15 minutes before using.*

TO FREEZE: *Before step 5, place an unrisen ball of dough in an individual resealable freezer bag to freeze for up to 1 month. To use, place the dough in the refrigerator the day before intended use or at room temperature 3 hours before intended use.*

Italian-Herbed Pizza Dough

MAKES 2 (12- TO 14-INCH) PIZZAS OR 4 PERSONAL PIZZAS

Inspired by the seasoning jars parked on pizza shop counters, this crust is a surprising way to add another layer of flavor to pizza. This pie will leave your kitchen aromatic with dried oregano, onion powder, and garlic, and you can complement the dried herbs by using the same fresh herbs to top the pizza. This is sure to be a favorite of anyone who loves a take-out slice.

PREP TIME: 15 minutes
RISE TIME: 1½ hours
COOK TIME: None

1 package active dry yeast
1½ cups warm water (about 110°F)
2 tablespoons extra-virgin olive oil
3 garlic cloves, minced
1 teaspoon dried oregano
½ teaspoon dried basil
½ teaspoon onion powder
4 cups all-purpose flour, plus more for dusting
1½ teaspoons salt

1 In a medium bowl, add the yeast to the warm water and let bloom for about 10 minutes. Add the olive oil, garlic, oregano, basil, and onion powder.

2 In a food processor, pulse to blend the flour and salt. With the machine running, add the yeast mixture in a slow, steady stream. Turn the machine off as soon as the dough comes together. Turn the dough out onto a well-floured board and, with lightly floured hands, knead the dough using the heels of your hands, pushing the dough and then folding it over. Shape into a ball and cut into 2 or 4 pieces.

3 Place the balls on a lightly floured pan and cover with a kitchen towel. Let the dough rise until it doubles in volume, about 1½ hours.

TO USE LATER: *Before step 3, place the balls of dough in individual resealable bags and refrigerate overnight. Let them stand at room temperature for 15 minutes before using.*

TO FREEZE: *Before step 3, place an unrisen ball of dough in an individual resealable bag to freeze for up to 1 month. To use, place the dough in the refrigerator the day before intended use or let it sit and rise at room temperature for 1½ hours before use.*

SAUCES & CONDIMENTS

Any meal is easily made when you've got a few flavorful building blocks in the fridge. All of the recipes in this chapter are perfect for spreading or scattering on pizza dough, but they can also be used in other applications. For instance, Basil Pesto (page 44), Black Olive Tapenade (page 45), and Oven-Roasted Cherry Tomatoes (page 49) are delicious over pasta or spread on toast with ricotta cheese. Cashew Cheese (page 43) is a great dairy-free cheese alternative for all sorts of dishes. And Balsamic-Roasted Garlic (page 46) or Quick-Pickled Red Onions (page 47) can add texture and unexpected flavor to salads and cheese plates.

Make a few of these sauces and condiments ahead, and you'll have plenty of options to choose from on pizza night. Just set them out on the counter with bowls of grated cheese, and let everyone dream up their own unique flavor combinations.

New York–Style Pizza Sauce

MAKES 1 QUART

Quick-cooked, this sauce has just a hint of depth and texture from garlic, onions, and a brief reduction. Highly spreadable, this sauce is meant to coat pizza dough with a spoon, so it has a thinner nature than pasta sauce. Add a tablespoon of tomato paste if you prefer it to have more body.

▼

GLUTEN-FREE

▼

NUT-FREE

▼

VEGAN

PREP TIME: 10 minutes
COOK TIME: 25 minutes

2 tablespoons extra-virgin olive oil
1 small yellow onion, chopped (½ cup)
3 garlic cloves, smashed
1 (28-ounce) can whole peeled San Marzano
    tomatoes, undrained
1 teaspoon fine sea salt
⅛ teaspoon freshly ground black pepper
1 to 2 tablespoons sugar

1 In a large saucepan over medium-high heat, heat the olive oil until it shimmers. Reduce the heat to medium and add the chopped onion. Cook, stirring occasionally, for 5 minutes. Add the garlic and continue to cook for 2 to 3 minutes more, until the onion is translucent and the garlic is aromatic.

2 Add the tomatoes and their juice, and bring to a simmer, stirring occasionally with a wooden spoon to break them apart. Simmer for 10 to 15 minutes, until the sauce has thickened.

3 Using an immersion blender or food processor, pulse until the sauce is smooth. Season with the salt, pepper, and sugar.

Cooking with kids: *Children generally prefer a smooth sauce to a chunky one, so let them handle the immersion blender. If they're so inclined, they can eradicate all recognizable tomato flesh!*

No-Cook Pizza Sauce

MAKES 1 QUART

There are days, particularly in summer, when an uncooked sauce feels right. This one breathes a little bit of seasoning into canned tomatoes and purées them into a chunky, rustic, convenient pizza topping. A can-to-table sauce is about simplicity and the sweet, bright essence of tomatoes.

GLUTEN-FREE

NUT-FREE

▼
VEGAN

PREP TIME: 10 minutes
COOK TIME: None

1 (28-ounce) can whole peeled San Marzano tomatoes, undrained

6 garlic cloves, chopped

2 teaspoons balsamic vinegar

½ teaspoon fine sea salt

⅛ teaspoon freshly ground black pepper

2 teaspoons extra-virgin olive oil

In the work bowl of a food processor, purée the tomatoes and their juice together with the garlic, vinegar, salt, pepper, and olive oil until smooth, stopping to scrape down the bowl as necessary.

A CLOSER LOOK: *San Marzano tomatoes are plum tomatoes grown in Italy. Their flavor and low seed count make them particularly suitable for sauces.*

White Sauce

Choose this classic béchamel for pizzas featuring chicken or roasted vegetables. This sauce can be made ahead, refrigerated, and gently heated over a medium-low heat before use. For a flavor-enriched version, add a few cloves of Balsamic-Roasted Garlic (page 46) and purée in a blender. Fantastique!

NUT-FREE

VEGETARIAN

PREP TIME: 5 minutes
COOK TIME: 20 minutes

3 tablespoons unsalted butter
3 tablespoons all-purpose flour
2 cups whole milk, heated until warm but not hot
½ teaspoon salt
⅛ teaspoon freshly ground black pepper

1 In a medium saucepan over medium heat, melt the butter. When it foams, add the flour and whisk to form a smooth paste. Continue to cook for 5 minutes, stirring frequently, until the mixture deepens in color.

2 Add the heated milk in half-cup increments, whisking in each to incorporate and cooking briefly before adding the next. When all the milk has been added, raise the heat to medium-high and continue whisking until the thickened sauce just begins to bubble, about 10 minutes. Remove from the heat.

3 Season with the salt and pepper. Keep at room temperature if using, or refrigerate if making ahead.

COOKING TIP: *Be sure to stir in the crease of the pan so none of the mixture burns. Use a wooden spoon occasionally to ensure that the entire pan is being stirred.*

Cashew Cheese

MAKES 1½ CUPS

For those who avoid dairy, cashew cheese is one of the best options for adding a creamy texture to pizza. This can be made while dough is rising, or stored covered in the refrigerator for up to a week. To top your pizza, spoon on the Cashew Cheese before baking, forming cheese-like trails that mimic the placement of mozzarella.

▼
GLUTEN-FREE
▼
VEGAN

PREP TIME: 25 minutes to 1 hour
COOK TIME: None

1 cup raw cashews
¼ cup water
¼ cup nutritional yeast
2 tablespoons freshly squeezed lemon juice
2 garlic cloves, peeled
1 tablespoon Dijon mustard

1 In a medium bowl, soak the cashews in the water for at least 20 minutes, or up to an hour.

2 In a blender, purée the soaked cashews and their liquid together with the yeast, lemon juice, garlic, and mustard. Blend until thick, creamy, and, depending on your preference, smooth.

Adventurous addition: *Add fresh herbs to the mix or even 2 tablespoons of white wine.*

Basil Pesto

MAKES 2 CUPS

Butter is the surprising but superstar addition to this recipe. It's the secret to a richly smooth, bright green blend of basil, cheese, and nuts, a mouthwatering topping for pizza as well as a beautiful one. Plus, there's nothing more uplifting than the smell of a kitchen where pesto is being made.

GLUTEN-FREE

VEGETARIAN

PREP TIME: 10 minutes
COOK TIME: None

¼ cup extra-virgin olive oil,
   plus more for covering

¼ cup walnuts

2 tablespoons pine nuts

½ garlic clove

¼ teaspoon salt

2 cups tightly packed fresh basil leaves,
   washed and dried

½ cup finely grated Parmesan cheese

1 tablespoon butter, at room temperature

1 In a food processor or blender, pulse to combine the olive oil, walnuts, pine nuts, garlic, and salt until smooth, stopping the machine as necessary to scrape down.

2 Add the basil in small handfuls, pulsing after each addition until smooth. When all of the basil has been incorporated, transfer to a medium mixing bowl. Add the grated Parmesan and the butter, mixing well to combine.

3 Cover with half an inch of extra-virgin olive oil, and store, refrigerated, for up to 3 days. Let come to room temperature before using.

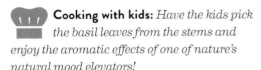 **Cooking with kids:** *Have the kids pick the basil leaves from the stems and enjoy the aromatic effects of one of nature's natural mood elevators!*

Black Olive Tapenade

MAKES 1½ CUPS

In the quest to bring balance to pizza toppings, depth and salt can be key ingredients. This tapenade adds both. The brininess of olives and capers, along with their striking color, brings out the brightness in whatever they're paired with. For a distinctly grown-up pizza, pair this sauce with goat cheese, arugula, and cocktails, or spoon a bit into salad dressings, especially if the salad features citrus. Use salt sparingly in other ingredients if using this tapenade.

GLUTEN-FREE

NUT-FREE

VEGAN

PREP TIME: 4 minutes
COOK TIME: None

½ pound black Gaeta olives, pitted
2 tablespoons capers, drained
1 garlic clove, peeled
Pinch red pepper flakes
¼ cup extra-virgin olive oil

1 In a food processor or blender, pulse the olives, capers, garlic, and red pepper flakes until blended. Add the olive oil and pulse to form a coarse paste.

2 Refrigerate, covered, for up to a week.

A CLOSER LOOK: *Gaeta olives from Rome are prized for their dark violet flesh and slightly tart flavor. Niçoise or Kalamata olives would be good substitutes.*

Balsamic-Roasted Garlic

MAKES 1 CUP

A seriously addictive take on oven-roasted garlic, this adds a mellow edge to almost anything; mix into mayonnaise, purée into potatoes, and, for a richly satisfying vegetarian pizza, toss a few cloves of Balsamic-Roasted Garlic with roasted butternut squash (see page 135 for roasting a butternut squash) and arugula. The mellow cloves are meltingly tender with just the right amount of acidic heat.

PREP TIME: 10 minutes
COOK TIME: 40 minutes

Cloves from 3 heads garlic, peeled (about 2 cups)
½ cup balsamic vinegar
2 tablespoons extra-virgin olive oil
1 tablespoon water

1 Preheat the oven to 350°F. Line a baking sheet with aluminum foil.

2 Spread the peeled garlic cloves on the prepared baking sheet.

3 In a small bowl, mix the balsamic vinegar, olive oil, and water. Spoon half of the mixture over the garlic cloves, tossing them to coat.

4 Bake for 30 minutes, stirring occasionally. Spoon the remaining vinegar mixture over the garlic and bake for 10 minutes more.

5 Refrigerate the garlic in an airtight container for up to 5 days. Bring to room temperature before using.

INGREDIENT TIP: *Don't bother using best quality balsamic vinegar here, as it's going to cook away.*

Quick-Pickled Red Onions

MAKES 2 CUPS

These pickled red onions are one of the simplest but most delicious ways to brighten pizza, sandwiches, and salads. With just a little hint of crunch, the sweet/sour mix of vinegar and sugar combined with the softly peppery bite of the onion is a crave-worthy combination.

PREP TIME: 10 minutes, plus 1 hour to rest
COOK TIME: None

½ cup apple cider vinegar

1 tablespoon sugar

½ teaspoon salt

1 large red onion, halved lengthwise and cut into thin half moons

1 In a large jar or other container with a lid, combine the vinegar, sugar, and salt. Stir until the sugar and salt are dissolved, then add the onions, pushing them down until they are completely submerged in the liquid.

2 Seal the container and let it rest at room temperature for at least 1 hour before using or refrigerating.

A CLOSER LOOK: *Pickling is the process of preserving food in vinegar or brine. This recipe uses a "quick pickling" method. While some pickles can last a year, these onions should be used within 2 weeks. Be sure to strain the onions before using—the liquid brine is not a desirable pizza topping!*

Sweet Onion Jam

Onions, burnished by a slow sauté, add a deep molten sweetness to pizza and are always amongst the most popular toppings. This is a simple recipe, but keep an eye on the pan. The onions should move from translucent to amber to deep brown. Keep them moving so it happens cohesively.

PREP TIME: 10 minutes
COOK TIME: 25 minutes

¼ cup extra-virgin olive oil

3 large Vidalia or yellow onions, halved lengthwise and cut into half moons

¼ teaspoon salt

⅛ teaspoon freshly ground black pepper

¾ cup white balsamic vinegar

1 In a large sauté pan over medium-high heat, heat the oil until it shimmers.

2 Add the onions, toss well to coat, and season with the salt and pepper. Reduce the heat to medium and cook, stirring frequently, until the onions are golden brown, 15 to 20 minutes.

3 Add the vinegar and raise the heat to medium-high to bring the liquid to a simmer. Cook, stirring frequently, until the vinegar has almost entirely evaporated, about 4 minutes.

4 Cool, transfer to a jar, and refrigerate for up to 3 days.

COOKING TIP: *During the cooking process, hot spots can form where onions begin to brown too quickly, which can lead to burning. If that happens, drizzle a little water over the spot and stir. This will halt the process and the water will evaporate.*

Oven-Roasted Cherry Tomatoes

MAKES 2 CUPS

This roasted tomato sauce makes for a deeply delicious and textural pizza. Partner it with smoked mozzarella and basil for an updated Margherita. Like many of the recipes in this chapter, these tomatoes are also a fabulous addition to brunch-time omelets.

PREP TIME: 5 minutes
COOK TIME: 30 minutes

3 tablespoons extra-virgin olive oil

3 pints cherry tomatoes

3 garlic cloves, peeled

2 fresh thyme sprigs, stemmed

2 tablespoons chopped fresh basil

½ teaspoon salt

¼ teaspoon freshly ground black pepper

1 Preheat the oven to 400°F.

2 On a parchment-lined baking sheet, toss the olive oil, cherry tomatoes, garlic, thyme, and basil. Season with the salt and pepper.

3 Bake for 30 minutes, gently tossing the tomatoes halfway through.

4 Scrape the roasted tomatoes into a large bowl, and stir until they form a chunky sauce.

5 The tomatoes can be refrigerated in an airtight container for up to 1 day.

 Adventurous addition: *While the tomatoes are roasting, prepare a simple stove-top agrodolce sauce to give them a sweet and sour zing. In a small saucepan, heat 1 tablespoon olive oil, add 1 tablespoon minced shallot, and cook until translucent. Add ¼ cup honey. When the honey bubbles, add 4 tablespoons good-quality red wine vinegar and cook until the liquid reduces. Pour the agrodolce over the finished tomatoes, and toss.*

Peperonata

MAKES 1½ CUPS

A cheerful little condiment, this Italian classic of oven-roasted red peppers adds color and depth to any pizza it meets. With depth and acidity, peperonata provides counterbalance to fresh cheeses and brings out the best in cured meats. For a simple but sublime snack, serve with Burrata cheese and a good crusty bread.

PREP TIME: 10 minutes
COOK TIME: 25 minutes

4 red bell peppers, cut into 1-inch dice
2 tablespoons extra-virgin olive oil
2 tablespoons balsamic vinegar
2 teaspoons dried thyme
Pinch red pepper flakes
¼ teaspoon salt

1 Preheat the oven to 350°F.

2 In a large bowl, toss the bell peppers, olive oil, vinegar, thyme, red pepper flakes, and salt to coat.

3 Transfer to a rimmed baking sheet or a 9-inch ovenproof skillet, and bake for 25 minutes, stirring with a spatula every 5 minutes, until the peppers are soft and tender.

4 Remove the baking sheet or skillet from the oven and transfer the peperonata to a bowl; let it cool to room temperature before using.

5 The peperonata can be refrigerated in an airtight container for up to 3 days.

 Adventurous addition: *Add smoky depth with ¾ teaspoon Spanish smoked paprika in step 2.*

Chili Oil

MAKES 1 CUP

Infused oils are a more penetrating way to deliver flavor. This one is a must for devotees of heat, for whom no meal is complete without a little fire. Drizzle it on pizza, either before or after baking, especially with sweet sausage and mozzarella. Drizzle a few drops onto a freshly cooked pasta dish or over oven-roasted broccoli, in place of plain olive oil.

GLUTEN-FREE

NUT-FREE

▼

VEGAN

PREP TIME: 2 minutes
COOK TIME: 3 minutes

1 cup extra-virgin olive oil
1 to 2 teaspoons red pepper flakes

1 In a small saucepan over medium-low heat, heat the olive oil and red pepper flakes for 3 minutes. Remove the pan from the heat and let the oil cool to room temperature.

2 Transfer the cooled oil to a squeeze bottle or a clean jar with a lid. Refrigerate for up to 1 month.

COOKING TIP: *Not hot enough? Add a whole dried chile to the pan. Swirl the whole pepper, or for more heat, slice it open and release the fiery seeds into the mix. Strain before using.*

Seasonal Spotlight: Spring

In spring pizza turns elegant when topped with young garlic and peas, whisper-thin prosciutto, or fresh crab or shrimp. Artichokes, spring onion, pancetta, and fresh ricotta make a fragrant, beautiful combination. Devour the excitement of what seems to be the shortest of all seasons by seeking out as many spring-only ingredients as possible. Look for ramps, radishes, fava beans, garlic scapes, and pea shoots, and partner them with shaved Parmesan and the most fragrant extra-virgin olive oils.

Asparagus, Cherry Tomato & Pine Nut Pizza

MAKES 2 (12- TO 14-INCH) PIZZAS
OR 4 PERSONAL PIZZAS

PREP TIME: 10 minutes
COOK TIME: 30 minutes
TOTAL TIME: 45 minutes

Cornmeal or flour, for dusting
1 tablespoon extra-virgin olive oil,
    plus more for brushing
¼ teaspoon salt, plus more for seasoning
1 bunch asparagus, tough ends snapped off
    and discarded
¼ cup pine nuts
⅛ teaspoon freshly ground black pepper
Simply Amazing Pizza Dough (page 25)
8 ounces fresh mozzarella cheese, shredded
1 cup Oven-Roasted Cherry Tomatoes (page 49)
12 fresh basil leaves, snipped with scissors

1 Preheat the oven and pizza stone (if using) to 500°F. Dust a pizza peel with cornmeal (if using a pizza stone), or brush two baking sheets with olive oil.

2 Bring a large pot of salted water to a boil. Blanch the asparagus for 3 minutes, and transfer to a large bowl of ice water to stop the cooking process. Cut the stalks into thirds on the diagonal. In a medium bowl, drizzle the cut asparagus with the olive oil, and season with salt and pepper.

3 In a small skillet over medium-low heat, toast the pine nuts until fragrant, about 2 minutes, swirling the pan frequently to prevent burning. Remove the skillet from the heat and set aside to cool.

4 Roll and stretch one of the dough balls to the desired size and place it on the pizza peel (if using a pizza stone) or on the prepared baking sheet. Transfer the dough to the pizza stone or oven rack, and bake for 2 to 3 minutes, until the dough just begins to brown at the edges. Transfer the dough to a cutting board, and flip it over.

5 Leaving a 1-inch border, spread half of the cheese over the browned side of the crust, followed by half of the Oven-Roasted Cherry Tomatoes and asparagus.

6 Return the pizza to the oven and bake until the crust is golden and the cheese has melted, 5 to 7 minutes on a pizza stone or 7 to 10 minutes on a baking sheet.

7 Transfer the pizza to the cutting board and top with half of the toasted pine nuts and snipped basil leaves. Let it rest for 5 minutes, then slice and serve.

8 Repeat with the remaining dough ball and toppings.

 Cooking with kids: *Blanch the asparagus ahead of time, and then let the kids assemble this one on their own.*

PARLOR CLASSICS

4

Half pepperoni, half plain—my pizza order remains steadfast. The kids insist on pepperoni, but I like the freedom of "plain." I resuscitate my side of the pie with whatever fresh little bits I've got on hand: Fried red peppers, caramelized onions, or a few folded-over slices of prosciutto give it a half-homemade lift of freshness.

When making pizza at home, I find that family and friends return again and again to the pizza toppings they grew up with. No matter how exciting toppings like kale, guanciale, or maitake mushrooms might be, the iconic parlor classics—the first words of our pizza vocabulary—remain on the tips of our tongues.

The parlor classics in this chapter use the packaged, low-moisture mozzarella that can be found in supermarkets and on classic New York–style slices. Grate it using the large holes of a box grater.

Simple Pepperoni Pizza

MAKES 2 (12-INCH) PIZZAS OR 4 PERSONAL PIZZAS

Devotees love the smoky-hot sweetness of America's most popular pizza topping. The spicy oil released by the heat of the oven is part of the appeal. You can buy pepperoni pre-sliced from a local butcher or specialty market. Don't forget the dried oregano and red pepper flakes for serving.

NUT-FREE

PREP TIME: 5 minutes
COOK TIME: 20 minutes
TOTAL TIME: 30 minutes

Cornmeal or flour, for dusting, or extra-virgin olive oil, for brushing
Simply Amazing Pizza Dough (page 25)
1 cup New York–Style Pizza Sauce (page 40)
1 cup grated mozzarella cheese
6 ounces pepperoni, sliced thin
¼ teaspoon salt

1 Preheat the oven and pizza stone (if using) to 500°F. Dust a pizza peel with cornmeal (if using a pizza stone), or brush two baking sheets with olive oil.

2 Roll out one of the dough balls and place it on the prepared peel or baking sheet.

3 Leaving a 1-inch border, spread half of the sauce evenly over the dough. Top with half the mozzarella and then half the pepperoni. Sprinkle with half the salt.

4 Transfer the pizza to the hot pizza stone or oven rack, and bake until the crust is golden and the cheese has melted, 5 to 7 minutes on the pizza stone or 7 to 10 minutes on the baking sheet.

5 Remove the pizza from the oven and transfer it to a cutting board. Let it rest for 5 minutes, then slice and serve.

6 Repeat with the remaining dough ball and toppings.

COOKING TIP: *The ratio of pizza to pepperoni is deeply personal and highly debated. I find 3 rounds of pepperoni per slice ideal, but for those who prefer heavier coverage, go for it!*

Sicilian Pizza

MAKES 1 (13-BY-18-INCH) PAN PIZZA

Sicilian Pizza is thicker and somewhat saucier than a regular slice. It tends to be the answer over a regular pizza when everyone is extra-hungry and in need of some pizza comfort. Baked in a pan, it's a simple pizza to make, requiring no skills with the pizza peel.

PREP TIME: 10 minutes
COOK TIME: 10 minutes
TOTAL TIME: 25 minutes

2 cups New York–Style Pizza Sauce (page 40)
No-Knead Pan Pizza Dough (page 32)
1½ cups grated mozzarella cheese
½ cup shredded provolone cheese
12 slices soppressata

1 Preheat the oven to 500°F.

2 Leaving a 1-inch border, spread the sauce evenly onto the dough.

3 In a medium bowl, toss together the mozzarella and provolone cheeses; sprinkle this mixture over the pizza. Top with the soppressata, 4 slices across and 3 slices down, ensuring that each slice of pizza is topped with one.

4 Transfer the baking pan to the preheated oven, and bake until the crust is golden and the cheese has melted, 7 to 10 minutes, rotating the pan halfway through.

5 Remove the pizza from the oven and let it rest for 5 minutes.

6 Run a spatula around the edges of the pan to loosen the pizza, slice, and serve.

Cooking with kids: *Pan pizzas, because of their dimensions, are especially adaptable to differing tastes. If there are pizza battles involving too much cheese or not enough sauce, let the kids have half the pizza to top exactly as they like.*

Sausage, Pepper & Onion Pizza

MAKES 2 (12-INCH) PIZZAS OR 4 PERSONAL PIZZAS

For ten days in September, the smell of sausage, peppers, and onions envelops the New York City neighborhood of Little Italy. The feast of San Gennaro, the patron saint of Naples, is a massive street fair and a tradition I never miss. For our family, it's an annual binge on way too much pizza, cannoli, and zeppole. I adore it as part of the city's romantic past. The unmistakable blend of frying peppers and onions reminds me of September nights on Mulberry Street. This classic combo is a little bit sweet and a little bit spicy.

PREP TIME: 10 minutes
COOK TIME: 40 minutes
TOTAL TIME: 55 minutes

Cornmeal or flour, for dusting

3 tablespoons extra-virgin olive oil, plus more as needed

¾ pound sweet Italian sausage (3 sausages)

1 medium yellow onion, sliced

1 red bell pepper, cut into ½-inch strips

1 green bell pepper, cut into ½-inch strips

2 garlic cloves, minced

¼ teaspoon red pepper flakes

Simply Amazing Pizza Dough (page 25) or Pro Dough (page 27)

New York–Style Pizza Sauce (page 40)

1⅓ cups grated mozzarella cheese

1 teaspoon fine sea salt

⅛ teaspoon freshly ground black pepper

½ teaspoon dried oregano

1 Preheat the oven and pizza stone (if using) to 500°F. Dust a pizza peel with cornmeal (if using a pizza stone), or brush two baking sheets with olive oil.

2 In a large skillet over medium heat, heat the olive oil until it shimmers. Add the sausages and cook until they are browned on all sides and register 160°F on an instant-read thermometer, about 8 minutes total. Transfer to a cutting board.

3 Add the onion to the hot pan (adding more oil if necessary), and sauté over medium heat until translucent, about 4 minutes. Add the red and green bell peppers. Sauté the mixture until the onions turn golden, about 4 minutes more, and then add the garlic and red pepper flakes. Cook, stirring, for about 2 additional minutes to infuse the mixture with the garlic. Using a slotted spoon, transfer the mixture to a small bowl.

4 Cut the sausages into ¼-inch-thick slices.

5 Roll out one of the dough balls to the desired size, and place it on the prepared peel or baking sheet.

6 Leaving a 1-inch border, spread half of the sauce evenly over the dough. Sprinkle half of the grated mozzarella over the pizza and then arrange half of the sausage slices on top. Spread half of the peppers and onions evenly over all.

7 Bake until the cheese has melted and the crust has browned, 5 to 7 minutes on the pizza stone or 7 to 10 minutes on the baking sheet.

8 Transfer the pizza to a cutting board and season with the salt, pepper, and dried oregano. Let it rest for 5 minutes, then slice and serve.

9 Repeat with the remaining dough ball and toppings.

PREP TIP: *Steps 2, 3, and 4 can be done the day before. Refrigerate the cooked peppers, onion, and sausage in an airtight container.*

Cooking with kids: *This is a no-fail sauté. Ask the kids to mind the stove (as you stand nearby) and watch as the onions and peppers melt down into a mellow sweetness.*

Spinach & Mushroom Pizza

MAKES 2 (12- TO 14-INCH) PIZZAS OR 4 PERSONAL PIZZAS

The difference between takeout and homemade is loud and clear in this classic vegetable pairing. Sautéing takes mere minutes, but the spinach remains bright and the mushrooms flavorful, and together they're a balanced, savory duo rather than a soggy, murky shadow of their former fresh selves. On the occasions that I do order a plain cheese pizza for delivery, I still make this topping fresh, bringing life to the slice. This classic parlor version features mozzarella cheese, but ricotta would be delicious, too.

▼

NUT-FREE

▼

VEGETARIAN

PREP TIME: 10 minutes
COOK TIME: 30 minutes
TOTAL TIME: 45 minutes

Cornmeal or flour, for dusting
4 tablespoons extra-virgin olive oil, divided,
    plus more for brushing
2 cups sliced cremini mushrooms
¼ teaspoon fine sea salt
⅛ teaspoon freshly ground black pepper
1 garlic clove
Pinch red pepper flakes, plus more for seasoning
4 cups baby spinach, stems removed
Simply Amazing Pizza Dough (page 25)
    or Pro Dough (page 27)
1 cup New York–Style Pizza Sauce (page 40)
1 cup grated mozzarella cheese

1 Preheat the oven and pizza stone (if using) to 500°F. Dust a pizza peel with cornmeal (if using a pizza stone), or brush two baking sheets with olive oil.

2 In a large skillet over medium-high heat, heat 3 tablespoons of olive oil until it shimmers. Add the mushrooms and the salt, and let the mushrooms sit undisturbed for 2 minutes. Give the pan a shake and continue to cook for 3 minutes more, stirring occasionally, until the mushrooms have darkened in color but are still firm and vibrant. Season with the pepper and transfer to a medium bowl.

3 Reduce the heat to medium and add the remaining 1 tablespoon of olive oil, the garlic, and the red pepper flakes. Swirl the garlic and red pepper flakes to flavor the oil, then add the spinach. Use tongs to turn the spinach, watching it

decrease in volume. Cook the spinach for 2 to 3 minutes, until it's wilted but still has structure. Remove the skillet from the heat.

4 Roll out one of the dough balls to the desired size and place it on the prepared peel or baking sheet.

5 Leaving a 1-inch border, spoon half of the sauce evenly over the dough, then sprinkle on half of the mozzarella. Scatter half of the spinach over the pizza, followed by half of the mushrooms. The toppings should intermingle. Season with freshly ground black pepper or more red pepper flakes as desired.

6 Transfer the pizza to the hot pizza stone or oven rack, and bake until the crust is golden and the cheese has melted, 5 to 7 minutes on the pizza stone or 7 to 10 minutes on the baking sheet.

7 Remove the pizza from the oven and transfer it to a cutting board. Let it rest for 5 minutes, then slice and serve.

8 Repeat with the remaining dough ball and toppings.

COOKING TIP: *The spinach is cooked with very little oil, letting the heat wilt and evenly color the spinach without adding extra fat to the pizza.*

Hawaiian Pizza

MAKES 2 (12- TO 14-INCH) PIZZAS OR 4 PERSONAL PIZZAS

According to the *Toronto Sun*, pineapple pizza was first served in Canada in 1962, and even though it was Hawaiian in spirit only, it didn't take long for this unconventional pizza to become a quirky mainstay on parlor menus nationwide. Pizza snobs might not want to like it, but when it's good, it's really good! Quality smoked ham and fresh pineapple elevate the yin/yang of sweet and salty. Grill it outdoors to enhance the smokiness.

PREP TIME: 10 minutes
COOK TIME: 25 minutes
TOTAL TIME: 40 minutes

Cornmeal or flour, for dusting, or extra-virgin olive oil, for brushing

4 slices center-cut bacon

Simply Amazing Pizza Dough (page 25) or Pro Dough (page 27)

1 cup New York–Style Pizza Sauce (page 40)

1 cup grated mozzarella cheese

¼ pound smoked ham, cut into ½-inch dice

1 cup diced fresh pineapple

2 tablespoons grated Parmesan cheese

1 Preheat the oven and pizza stone (if using) to 500°F. Dust a pizza peel with cornmeal (if using a pizza stone), or brush two baking sheets with olive oil.

2 In a medium skillet over medium heat, cook the bacon until crisp, 2 to 3 minutes per side. Transfer to a paper towel–lined plate to cool. Cut into bits.

3 Roll out one of the dough balls to the desired size and place it on the pizza peel (if using a pizza stone) or on the prepared baking sheet.

4 Leaving a 1-inch border, spread half of the sauce evenly onto the dough. Sprinkle on half of the mozzarella, followed by half of the ham, chopped bacon, pineapple, and grated Parmesan cheese.

5 Transfer the pizza to the hot pizza stone or oven rack, and bake until the crust is golden and the cheese has melted, 5 to 7 minutes on the pizza stone or 7 to 10 minutes on the baking sheet.

6 Remove the pizza from the oven and transfer it to a cutting board. Let it rest for 5 minutes, then slice and serve.

7 Repeat with the remaining dough ball and toppings.

COOKING TIP: *Dry the diced pineapple with paper towels before placing it on the pizza to enable better browning and prevent the liquid from pooling on the pizza.*

Meatball Pizza

MAKES 2 (12- TO 14-INCH) PIZZAS OR 4 PERSONAL PIZZAS

Meatball pizza can be one of the most delicious pies, but the downside of the delivery version is that the meatballs, sliced and strewn like pepperoni, often dry out as the pizza cooks. Here, smaller meatballs are kept whole, remaining moist and flavorful.

▼
NUT-FREE

PREP TIME: 10 minutes
COOK TIME: 25 minutes
TOTAL TIME: 40 minutes

All-purpose flour, for dusting and coating
½ pound ground pork
½ pound ground veal
1 cup ricotta cheese
¼ cup grated Parmesan cheese
　　plus 2 tablespoons, divided
2 tablespoons finely chopped fresh flat-leaf parsley
¼ teaspoon salt, plus more for sprinkling
⅛ teaspoon freshly ground black pepper,
　　plus more for sprinkling
2½ cups New York–Style Pizza Sauce
　　(page 40), divided
2 tablespoons olive oil, plus more for brushing
Simply Amazing Pizza Dough (page 25)
2 cups grated mozzarella cheese

1 Preheat the oven and pizza stone (if using) to 500°F. Lightly flour a baking sheet.

2 In a large mixing bowl, use your hands to combine the ground pork and veal, ricotta, ¼ cup of Parmesan, and the parsley. Season with the salt and pepper, and mix again.

3 Form each meatball by rolling 1 heaping tablespoon of the meat mixture between your palms. Place the meatballs on the prepared baking sheet, lightly rolling each one in flour.

4 In a medium saucepan over medium heat, heat 1½ cups of sauce; let it come to a gentle simmer.

5 Meanwhile, in a large skillet over medium-high heat, heat the olive oil. When it shimmers, add the meatballs, cooking on all sides for about 3 minutes, until browned. As they brown, transfer the meatballs to the simmering sauce to finish cooking, about 5 minutes total.

6 Dust a pizza peel with cornmeal (if using a pizza stone), or brush two baking sheets with olive oil.

7 Roll out one of the dough balls to the desired size and place it on the pizza peel (if using a pizza stone) or on the prepared baking sheet.

8 Leaving a 1-inch border, spread ½ cup of the remaining sauce evenly onto the dough. Top the sauce with half of the mozzarella and half of the meatballs. Spoon a little extra sauce from the pan onto the pizza, and finish with 1 tablespoon of the remaining Parmesan cheese and a sprinkling of salt and pepper.

9 Transfer the pizza to the hot pizza stone or oven rack, and bake until the crust is golden and the cheese has melted, 5 to 7 minutes on the pizza stone or 7 to 10 minutes on the baking sheet.

10 Remove the pizza from the oven and transfer it to a cutting board. Let it rest for 5 minutes, then slice and serve.

11 Repeat from step 7 with the remaining dough ball and toppings.

SUBSTITUTION TIP: *Replace the ground beef with ground lamb for a more pronounced flavor.*

PREP TIP: *The meatballs can be cooked ahead of time and refrigerated in the sauce overnight.*

Four-Cheese Pizza

MAKES 2 (12- TO 14-INCH) PIZZAS OR 4 PERSONAL PIZZAS

This indulgent pie is a celebration of the subtlety of Parmesan, the meltability of mozzarella, and the edge and assertiveness that a blend of cheeses can deliver. And for the kids who eat nothing but bread and cheese (we all know them), a four-cheese, make-your-own pizza offers a chance to sprinkle a little of this, a little of that for a delicious step toward variety. This version features the tangy flavor of goat cheese and a smattering of fresh tomato. A little pesto drizzled over the top would be a nice boost of both flavor and color.

PREP TIME: 15 minutes
COOK TIME: 20 minutes
TOTAL TIME: 40 minutes

Cornmeal or flour, for dusting, or extra-virgin olive oil, for brushing
Simply Amazing Pizza Dough (page 25)
1 cup New York–Style Pizza Sauce (page 40)
¾ cup grated mozzarella or 6 ounces sliced fresh mozzarella cheese
¾ cup grated fontina cheese
2 plum tomatoes, sliced thin
⅓ cup crumbled goat cheese
½ cup Parmesan cheese
8 fresh basil leaves, torn or roughly chopped
1 tablespoon chopped fresh parsley
¼ teaspoon salt
⅛ teaspoon freshly ground black pepper

1 Preheat the oven and pizza stone (if using) to 500°F. Dust a pizza peel with cornmeal (if using a pizza stone), or brush two baking sheets with olive oil.

2 Roll out one of the dough balls to the desired size, and place it on the pizza peel (if using a pizza stone) or on the prepared baking sheet.

3 Leaving a 1-inch border, spread half of the sauce evenly over the dough. Sprinkle on half of the mozzarella and fontina. Arrange half of the tomato slices on top, and finish with half of the goat cheese and Parmesan.

4 Transfer the pizza to the hot pizza stone or oven rack, and bake until the crust is golden and the cheese has melted, 5 to 7 minutes on the pizza stone or 7 to 10 minutes on the baking sheet.

5 Remove the pizza from the oven and transfer it to a cutting board. Let it rest for 5 minutes, then top with half of the basil and parsley and season with half of the salt and pepper. Slice and serve.

6 Repeat with the remaining dough ball and toppings.

Keep it simple: *Replace the goat cheese with shredded provolone for a milder, more kid-friendly blend of cheeses.*

Meat Lover's Pizza

MAKES 2 (12- TO 14-INCH) PIZZAS OR 4 PERSONAL PIZZAS

A Meat Lover's pie can sometimes be an over-the-top display of carnivorous abandon, but the best ones are about the variety of meats rather than the excess. Cook the sausage and bacon in advance, and drain well before topping the pizza. It might be considered sacrilege, but I'm a fan of topping this pizza with a handful of arugula or any other salad, making it into a one-slice meal.

PREP TIME: 15 minutes
COOK TIME: 35 minutes
TOTAL TIME: 50 minutes

Cornmeal or flour, for dusting
Extra-virgin olive oil, for brushing and drizzling
4 slices center-cut bacon
4 slices prosciutto, cut into strips
½ pound sweet or hot Italian sausage, casings removed
Simply Amazing Pizza Dough (page 25) or Pro Dough (page 27)
1 cup New York–Style Pizza Sauce (page 40)
1½ cups grated mozzarella cheese
¼ cup thinly sliced pepperoni or soppressata
2 tablespoons chopped fresh flat-leaf parsley
½ teaspoon fine sea salt
¼ teaspoon freshly ground black pepper

1 Preheat the oven and pizza stone (if using) to 500°F. Dust a pizza peel with cornmeal (if using a pizza stone), or brush two baking sheets with olive oil.

2 In a medium skillet over medium heat, cook the bacon until crisp, 2 to 3 minutes per side. Transfer to a paper towel–lined plate and set aside to cool.

3 Add the prosciutto to the skillet and cook over medium heat for about 3 minutes, stirring constantly, until crisp. Transfer the prosciutto to the plate with the bacon. Chop the bacon and prosciutto into bite-size pieces.

4 If there's not enough bacon fat in the skillet to prevent sticking, add a drizzle of olive oil and return the skillet to medium heat. Add the sausage to the skillet and cook for about 5 minutes, stirring constantly and breaking it up with a wooden spoon, until no pink color remains. Use a slotted spoon to transfer the sausage to another paper towel–lined plate.

5 Roll out one of the dough balls to the desired size, and place it on the pizza peel (if using a pizza stone) or on the prepared baking sheet.

6 Leaving a 1-inch border, spread half of the sauce evenly onto the dough. Sprinkle on half of the mozzarella, then half of the sausage, bacon, and prosciutto. Finish with half of the pepperoni so that the meat forms a single, even layer.

7 Transfer the pizza to the hot pizza stone or oven rack and bake until the crust is golden and the pepperoni is sizzling, 5 to 7 minutes on the pizza stone or 7 to 10 minutes on the baking sheet.

8 Remove the pizza from the oven and transfer it to a cutting board. Let it rest for 5 minutes, then top with half of the chopped parsley, salt, and pepper. Slice and serve.

9 Repeat from step 5 with the remaining dough ball and toppings.

Adventurous addition: *A few strands of Quick-Pickled Red Onions (page 47) added either before or after cooking would give eye-opening textural contrast to the meats on this pizza, and a drizzle of good-quality balsamic vinegar over the finished pizza would definitely up its wow factor.*

Deep-Dish Pizza

MAKES 1 DEEP-DISH PIZZA

According to the BBC, deep-dish pizzas were created in 1943 Chicago by a restaurant that later became the Pizzeria Uno chain. While Chicago is famous for deep-dish, it's the square-cut slice that's most popular in the Windy City.

PREP TIME: 10 minutes, plus 10 minutes to chill
COOK TIME: 35 minutes
TOTAL TIME: 1 hour

1 tablespoon extra-virgin olive oil,
  plus more for greasing and drizzling
1 pound sweet or hot Italian sausage,
  casings removed
1 tablespoon chopped fresh flat-leaf parsley
All-purpose flour, for dusting
Deep-Dish Pizza Dough (page 36)
¾ pound mozzarella cheese, sliced
1 cup sautéed mushrooms (optional)
2 cups New York–Style Pizza Sauce (page 40)
1 cup freshly grated Parmesan cheese
½ teaspoon dried oregano
½ teaspoon dried thyme
¼ teaspoon coarse sea salt
⅛ teaspoon freshly ground black pepper

1 Preheat the oven to 425°F. Coat a 12-inch round cake pan or cast iron skillet with olive oil.

2 In a medium skillet over medium heat, heat the oil. Add the sausage and cook for about 5 minutes, stirring constantly and breaking it up with a wooden spoon, until no pink color remains. Use a slotted spoon to transfer the sausage to a paper towel–lined plate. Add the parsley and toss well to combine.

3 Place the dough on a lightly floured surface and roll it out into a 14-inch circle.

4 Transfer the dough to the prepared pan, stretching it so that its diameter exceeds the rim of the pan. If the dough shrinks after being stretched, place it in the refrigerator for 10 minutes. Continue stretching until the dough can be tucked into the crease of the pan and cover the sides, similar to pie dough. Pierce the dough in a few places with the tines of a fork, and refrigerate for 10 minutes.

5 Transfer the empty pizza crust to the preheated oven and bake for 10 minutes, or until it just begins to brown. Remove the crust from the oven.

6 Cover the bottom of the crust with the sliced mozzarella in an even layer. Spread the sausage-parsley mixture on top of the cheese, followed by the mushrooms (if using), and then the sauce. Sprinkle with the Parmesan, oregano, and thyme, drizzle lightly with olive oil, and sprinkle with the salt and pepper.

7 Bake the pizza for 25 minutes, until the filling is bubbling hot. Remove it from the oven and let it rest for 5 minutes. Use two spatulas to lift it out of the pan, slice, and serve.

COOKING TIP: *Deep-Dish Pizza can be made in a 12-inch round layer cake pan or a 12-inch skillet; no need to buy a special pan.*

Adventurous addition: *For something completely different, replace the sausage with $\frac{3}{4}$ pound ground lamb, browned and seasoned with 2 teaspoons ground cumin.*

Seasonal Spotlight: Summer

In the summertime, use vine-ripened heirloom tomatoes and backyard herbs as a starting point, then experiment with the season's freshest, most colorful produce on grilled pizzas. At the time of year when produce is at its freshest and most flavorful, the approach is simple: Let the grill do the work. Toppings are either grilled to bring out a smoky sweetness or raw to showcase their seasonal peak freshness.

Rely on farm-stand inspiration: clams with sweet corn, grilled peaches with Taleggio and pine nuts, or zucchini flowers with fresh ricotta. Eggplant, summer squash, and tender greens come together to make the easiest, most nutritious, best-looking pizzas of the year.

Roasted Corn & Smoky Eggplant Pizza

MAKES 2 (12- TO 14-INCH) PIZZAS OR 4 PERSONAL PIZZAS

Each summer I vow to learn to play the ukulele and eat locally grown sweet corn every day. I still can't play a tune, but I've developed countless ways to enjoy corn at almost every meal. Grilled corn adds a beautiful textural element to pizza and marries well with almost any cheese or topping. This pizza is a mix of the fresh summer vegetables that are almost always piled on my kitchen counter.

When the grill is going, I tend to do all of my prep and cooking outside. This pizza uses a "puréed" grilled eggplant as its base. Instead of using a food processer, I use a hand-chopped method. It's quieter and requires less cleanup.

PREP TIME: 25 minutes, plus 1 hour to preheat grill
COOK TIME: 35 minutes
TOTAL TIME: 2 hours, 5 minutes

NUT-FREE

VEGAN

3 (10-ounce) eggplants, trimmed and peeled

¼ teaspoon salt, plus more for seasoning

3 tablespoons extra-virgin olive oil, divided

6 ears corn, shucked

2 garlic cloves, minced

4 fresh thyme sprigs, stemmed

⅛ teaspoon freshly ground black pepper,
    plus more for seasoning

¼ teaspoon Hungarian smoked paprika

Simply Amazing Pizza Dough (page 25)
    or Pro Dough (page 27)

½ pint cherry tomatoes, halved

1 zucchini, ends trimmed, peeled,
    and thinly cut lengthwise into ribbons

1 Prepare a charcoal or propane grill as described on page 14 or use a grill pan on the stove.

2 Cut the eggplant lengthwise into ½-inch slices. Set a wire rack inside a rimmed baking sheet. Sprinkle the eggplant slices with the salt, and place them in a single layer on the prepared rack. Let them drain for 10 minutes. Pat them dry with paper towels.

3 Brush the eggplant slices with 2 tablespoons of olive oil, and grill them over high direct heat for 4 minutes per side. The eggplant slices should be lightly charred and tender. Return the grilled eggplant to the metal rack.

4 Rub the corn cobs lightly with the remaining 1 tablespoon of olive oil, and grill them for 3 to 4 minutes per side, until lightly charred. Using a chef's knife, cut the kernels away from the cob, catching them in a large bowl.

5 Using two chef's knives, chop the grilled eggplant, minced garlic, and thyme. Chop until the eggplant is a chunky purée. Use the blade of a knife to slide the purée into a large bowl. Season with salt, the pepper, and the smoked paprika. (If you'd prefer to do this in a food processor, pulse to a rough paste.)

6 Roll out one of the dough balls to the desired size.

7 Grill the dough over indirect high heat for 2 to 3 minutes per side, or until lightly charred.

8 Using tongs, transfer the crust to a cutting board. Spread half of the eggplant mixture over the crust, and top with half of the grilled corn, half of the cherry tomatoes, and a few ribbons of zucchini. Season with salt and pepper.

9 Return the pizza to the grill over indirect high heat, close the lid, and grill for 5 to 7 minutes or until the crust is golden and the tomatoes have collapsed and started to bubble.

10 Remove the pizza from the grill, and let it rest for 5 minutes. Slice and serve.

11 Repeat from step 6 with the remaining dough ball and toppings.

COOKING TIP: *Zucchini can give off liquid and make for a soggy pizza. For this pizza, the zucchini is treated more as a garnish than a topping. Thinly slice it into long ribbons and, as you would with fresh herbs, scatter a few over the pizza for texture and color.*

MEAT, POULTRY & SEAFOOD

Meatier pizzas should have the same balance of elements as a great sandwich: protein, melted cheese, crisp crust, and the fresh flavor of something green.

Pepperoni, sausage, and meatballs are the tried and true MVPs of meat pizza, but masterfully cured Italian meats—salumi such as bresaola, prosciutto, or coppa—and shredded chicken make for beautifully rustic pizzas, too.

Seafood pizzas come alive with a heavy dose of herbs. Like most kids who grew up in the Northeast, I encountered clam pizza at a young age and was surprised by the idea of it. These days it's more commonly found, along with other seafood toppings like scallops, smoked mussels, shrimp, and tuna. Served with fresh corn and parsley or basil, these are some of my summer favorites. And any time of year, anchovies make for a sophisticated pizza topping with sautéed onions and black olives.

Grilled Skirt Steak Caprese Pizza

MAKES 2 (12- TO 14-INCH) PIZZAS OR 4 PERSONAL PIZZAS

This is a crowd-pleaser, especially in summer months when the grill is in full effect. I see the crust more as a flatbread in this, a base for an open-face steak sandwich. With easy-to-make skirt steak and a rainbow of heirloom tomatoes, it's what I think of when I want a simple, meat-based dinner on a pizza—a magnificent one-slice meal.

PREP TIME: 15 minutes, plus 8 hours to marinate
COOK TIME: 30 minutes
TOTAL TIME: 8 hours, 55 minutes

For the steak
2 tablespoons Dijon mustard
½ cup extra-virgin olive oil
¼ cup Worcestershire sauce
3 tablespoons soy sauce
4 garlic cloves, smashed
1 pound skirt steak
2 fresh rosemary sprigs, stemmed
2 fresh thyme sprigs, stemmed
½ teaspoon salt
¼ teaspoon freshly ground black pepper

For the pizza
Simply Amazing Pizza Dough (page 25)
    or Pro Dough (page 27)
2 pinches dried oregano
6 ounces fresh mozzarella cheese, grated
1 pound heirloom tomatoes, sliced thin
8 fresh basil leaves, torn
4 handfuls arugula
2 tablespoons extra-virgin olive oil
¼ teaspoon fine sea salt
⅛ teaspoon freshly ground black pepper

To prepare the steak

1 In a small bowl, whisk the mustard, olive oil, Worcestershire, soy sauce, and garlic until well combined.

2 Place the steak in a casserole dish, pour the marinade over it, and scatter on the rosemary and thyme. Cover and refrigerate for 8 hours or overnight, turning the meat once or twice.

3 Heat an outdoor grill or a grill pan on the stove to high heat. Remove the steak from the marinade and season on both

sides with the salt and pepper. Grill the steak for 5 minutes per side for medium rare. Remove the steak from the grill, and transfer it to a cutting board. Let it rest for 5 to 10 minutes, then slice it thinly against the grain.

To make the pizza

1 Preheat an outdoor grill to indirect high heat (see page 14 for grilling instructions), or preheat the oven and pizza stone (if using) to 500°F.

2 Roll out one of the dough balls to the desired size, and place it on the pizza peel (if using a pizza stone) or on the prepared baking sheet. If you're grilling the pizza, brown the dough on both sides (see page 14).

3 Sprinkle the dough with half of the dried oregano, then top with half of the shredded fresh mozzarella followed by half of the tomato slices. Garnish with half of the torn basil leaves.

4 Transfer the pizza to the grill, hot pizza stone, or oven rack, and grill or bake until the crust is golden and the cheese has melted, 5 to 7 minutes on the grill or pizza stone or 7 to 10 minutes on the baking sheet.

5 Remove the pizza from the grill or oven and transfer it to a cutting board. Top the pizza with half of the arugula and sliced steak. Drizzle half of the oil over the pizza and sprinkle on half of the salt and pepper. Slice and serve.

6 Repeat from step 2 with the remaining dough ball and toppings.

PREP TIP: *You can grill the steak up to 2 days ahead. Just leave it unsliced and let it cool completely at room temperature, then transfer to an airtight container and refrigerate. When you're ready to make the pizza, slice the steak thinly against the grain.*

Cooking with kids: *Arranging multicolored, multisize heirloom tomatoes is an art unto itself, perfect for small abstract expressionists.*

Pulled Pork, Brussels Sprouts & Purple Cabbage Pizza

MAKES 2 (12- TO 14-INCH) PIZZAS OR 4 PERSONAL PIZZAS

Pulled pork is such a prized leftover that it makes all kinds of sense to cook a big batch on Sunday to use for lunches and dinners during the week. The meat can then top a hearty pizza with pan-roasted Brussels sprouts, a surprising favorite vegetable of many kids. If you can find small Brussels sprouts, then you don't have to separate the leaves. Just trim them and cut them in half lengthwise.

PREP TIME: 15 minutes
COOK TIME: 8 hours, 30 minutes
TOTAL TIME: 8 hours, 50 minutes

For the pulled pork
1 tablespoon chili powder
1 tablespoon fine sea salt
½ teaspoon cayenne pepper
½ teaspoon cumin
1 tablespoon packed brown sugar
1 (4-pound) boneless pork shoulder
    (or Boston butt)
2 medium yellow onions, sliced
4 garlic cloves, smashed
1½ cups low-sodium chicken broth
1½ cups barbecue sauce

For the pizza
Cornmeal or flour, for dusting, or extra-virgin
    olive oil, for brushing
4 slices of center-cut bacon

½ pound Brussels sprouts, trimmed, leaves separated
¼ teaspoon fine sea salt
⅛ teaspoon freshly ground black pepper
Simply Amazing Pizza Dough (page 25)
    or Pro Dough (page 27)
¼ cup barbecue sauce
1 cup grated fontina cheese
1 cup grated pepper Jack cheese
¼ cup Quick-Pickled Red Onions (page 47)

To make the pulled pork

1 In a small bowl, mix together the chili powder, salt, cayenne, cumin, and brown sugar. Pat the meat dry with paper towels and rub it all over with the spice mixture.

2 Place the onions, garlic, and chicken broth in a slow cooker and add the spice-rubbed pork. Cook on low for 6 to 8 hours; the meat should be tender and falling apart. When the meat is finished cooking, discard the cooking liquid. Place the meat

in a large bowl and shred it using two forks. Then pour in the barbecue sauce and mix well until the shredded meat is fully coated.

To make the pizza

1 Preheat the oven and pizza stone (if using) to 500°F. Dust a pizza peel with cornmeal (if using a pizza stone), or brush two baking sheets with olive oil.

2 In a large skillet over medium-high heat, cook the bacon until crisp, about 7 minutes. Remove the skillet from the heat and transfer the bacon to a paper towel–lined plate. When the bacon is cool enough to handle, chop it into bite-size pieces.

3 Return the skillet to medium-high heat, add the Brussels sprout leaves, and season with the salt and pepper. Sauté for 3 to 5 minutes, or until wilted, then immediately remove the skillet from the heat and transfer the Brussels sprouts to a medium bowl. Add the bacon and toss well to combine.

4 Roll out one of the dough balls to the desired size, and place it on the pizza peel (if using a pizza stone) or on the prepared baking sheet.

5 Leaving a 1-inch border, brush the crust with half of the barbecue sauce, spreading it into a thin, even layer.

6 In a medium bowl, mix together the fontina and pepper Jack cheeses. Sprinkle half of the cheese mixture over the pizza, then top with half of the pulled pork and half of the Brussels sprouts and bacon.

7 Transfer the pizza to the hot pizza stone or oven rack, and bake until the crust is golden and the cheese has melted, 5 to 7 minutes on the pizza stone or 7 to 10 minutes on the baking sheet.

8 Remove the pizza from the oven and transfer it to a cutting board. Let it rest for 5 minutes, then top with half of the Quick-Pickled Red Onions. Slice and serve.

9 Repeat from step 4 with the remaining dough ball and toppings.

PREP TIP: *You can make the pulled pork up to 3 days ahead. After it is cooked, shredded, and coated in barbecue sauce, transfer it to an airtight container and refrigerate.*

 Cooking with kids: *Ask the kids to shred the pork and mix it with the barbecue sauce.*

Spicy Sausage Pizza with Peperonata & Red Onion

MAKES 2 (12- TO 14-INCH) PIZZAS OR 4 PERSONAL PIZZAS

▼
NUT-FREE

Peperonata is the softer side of red peppers. Its sweetness and deep color punctuate this richly flavored pizza, layered with white sauce and white cheese. If pizza is about simplicity, this one flirts with excess.

PREP TIME: 15 minutes
COOK TIME: 25 minutes
TOTAL TIME: 50 minutes

Cornmeal or flour, for dusting

1 tablespoon extra-virgin olive oil, plus more for brushing

2 hot Italian sausage links (about ½ pound), casings removed

Simply Amazing Pizza Dough (page 25)

¾ cup White Sauce (page 42)

2 garlic cloves, minced

¾ cup grated mozzarella cheese

3 tablespoons grated Parmesan cheese

¼ cup Peperonata (page 50)

1 small red onion, sliced thin

2 fresh oregano sprigs, stemmed and chopped

½ teaspoon fine sea salt

¼ teaspoon freshly ground black pepper

1 Preheat the oven and pizza stone (if using) to 500°F. Dust a pizza peel with cornmeal (if using a pizza stone), or brush two baking sheets with olive oil.

2 In a sauté pan over medium-high heat, heat the olive oil. Add the sausage and cook, breaking it up with a wooden spoon, until no longer pink, 4 to 6 minutes. Use a slotted spoon to transfer the cooked sausage to a medium bowl.

3 Roll out one of the dough balls to the desired size, and place it on the pizza peel (if using a pizza stone) or on the prepared baking sheet.

4 Leaving a 1-inch border, spoon half of the White Sauce evenly onto the dough. Sprinkle with half of the minced garlic, then top with half of the mozzarella and grated Parmesan. Finish with half of the Peperonata and red onion slices.

5 Transfer the pizza to the hot pizza stone or oven rack, and bake until the crust is golden and the cheese has melted, 5 to 7 minutes on the pizza stone or 7 to 10 minutes on the baking sheet.

6 Remove the pizza from the oven and transfer it to a cutting board. Let it rest for 5 minutes, then sprinkle with half of the oregano, salt, and pepper. Slice and serve.

7 Repeat from step 3 with the remaining dough ball and toppings.

Keep it simple: *To make this pie more kid-friendly, use sweet Italian sausage and offer the peperonata as an option.*

Chorizo Pizza with Prosciutto, Olives & Piquillo Peppers

MAKES 2 (12- TO 14-INCH) PIZZAS OR 4 PERSONAL PIZZAS

NUT-FREE

For those who love chorizo (and that seems to be almost everyone), it is an instantly recognizable flavor booster with a mild, smoky heat. This pizza pairs these flavorful sausages with piquillo peppers, another magnificent Spanish ingredient, creating a spicy warmth that is very kid friendly.

PREP TIME: 15 minutes
COOK TIME: 30 minutes
TOTAL TIME: 50 minutes

Cornmeal or flour, for dusting

2 tablespoons extra-virgin olive oil, plus extra for brushing

3 fresh chorizo sausage links

Simply Amazing Pizza Dough (page 25)

1 cup New York–Style Pizza Sauce (page 40)

1 cup grated mozzarella cheese

4 smoked piquillo peppers, drained and sliced lengthwise

4 slices prosciutto, torn into small pieces

¼ cup halved black olives

¼ cup chopped fresh flat-leaf parsley

½ cup grated manchego cheese

⅛ teaspoon freshly ground black pepper

1 Preheat the oven and pizza stone (if using) to 500°F. Dust a pizza peel with cornmeal (if using a pizza stone), or brush two baking sheets with olive oil.

2 In a medium skillet over medium heat, heat the oil until hot but not smoking. Add the sausages and cook for 7 to 10 minutes, turning occasionally, until they are browned on all sides. Remove the skillet from the heat and set it aside to cool. When the chorizo is cool enough to handle, cut it into thin slices.

3 Roll out one of the dough balls to the desired size, and place it on the pizza peel (if using a pizza stone) or on the prepared baking sheet.

4 Leaving a 1-inch border, spoon the sauce evenly onto the pizza. Top with half of the mozzarella cheese, followed by half of the piquillo peppers. Scatter half of the chorizo and prosciutto over the pizza, followed by half of the olives and parsley.

5 Transfer the pizza to the hot pizza stone or oven rack, and bake until the crust is golden and the cheese has melted, 5 to 7 minutes on the pizza stone or 7 to 10 minutes on the baking sheet.

6 Remove the pizza from the oven, transfer it to a cutting board, and let it rest for 5 minutes. Top with half of the manchego and pepper, slice, and serve.

7 Repeat from step 3 with the remaining dough ball and toppings.

A CLOSER LOOK: *Piquillo peppers are grown in northern Spain. They have a sweet, pleasant flavor and texture. If you can't find them in your local grocery store, you can use roasted red peppers instead.*

Keep it simple: *If chorizo isn't available, use sweet Italian sausage seasoned with a little smoked paprika. If the kids aren't fans of olives, serve the olives as a garnish alongside the cooked pizza.*

Prosciutto Cotto Pizza with Pesto & Spring Garlic

MAKES 2 (12- TO 14-INCH) PIZZAS OR 4 PERSONAL PIZZAS

Tender spring garlic (the young plant, picked before the bulb has formed) has a mellow beauty worth showcasing. It's one of the harbingers of spring at the farmers' market, and paired with prosciutto cotto, it makes for a seasonal garlic—lovers pizza that's a cut above.

PREP TIME: 10 minutes
COOK TIME: 20 minutes
TOTAL TIME: 35 minutes

Cornmeal or flour, for dusting, or extra-virgin olive oil, for brushing

Simply Amazing Pizza Dough (page 25)

4 stalks spring garlic or ramps, white and light green parts finely chopped, or 2 garlic cloves, sliced thin

¾ cup Basil Pesto (page 44)

½ pound fresh mozzarella cheese, shredded or cut into small pieces

¾ cup fresh ricotta cheese

¼ pound prosciutto cotto or Virginia ham, chopped into bite-size pieces

⅛ teaspoon salt

⅛ teaspoon freshly ground black pepper

1 Preheat the oven and pizza stone (if using) to 500°F. Dust a pizza peel with cornmeal (if using a pizza stone), or brush two baking sheets with olive oil.

2 Roll out one of the dough balls to the desired size, and place it on the pizza peel (if using a pizza stone) or on the prepared baking sheet.

3 Sprinkle half of the spring garlic over the dough, then spread half of the Basil Pesto on top evenly. Sprinkle on half of the mozzarella, dot the pizza with half of the ricotta, and finish with half of the ham.

4 Transfer the pizza to the hot pizza stone or oven rack, and bake until the crust is golden and the cheese has melted, 5 to 7 minutes on the pizza stone or 7 to 10 minutes on the baking sheet.

5 Remove the pizza from the oven and transfer it to a cutting board. Let it rest for 5 minutes, then season with the salt and pepper. Slice and serve.

6 Repeat with the remaining dough ball and toppings.

A CLOSER LOOK: *Prosciutto cotto, a cooked Italian ham, is a stand-out in sandwiches, panini, and this delicious pizza. If prosciutto cotto isn't available, any good-quality sliced ham will work.*

Alsatian Bacon & Onion Pizza

MAKES 1 PAN PIZZA

This is the opposite of healthy eating, but it's so tasty that the occasional indulgence is worth it—maybe even good for the soul. This pizza is inspired by the pizzas of Alsace, which are typically layered with fromage blanc. Crème fraîche and fromage blanc are soft, sweet white cheeses similar to cream cheese.

PREP TIME: 10 minutes
COOK TIME: 20 minutes
TOTAL TIME: 35 minutes

½ cup crème fraîche, at room temperature
1 cup fromage blanc, at room temperature
½ cup White Sauce (page 42)
2 pinches ground nutmeg
½ pound slab bacon (lardons), chopped into bite-size pieces
1 medium white onion, sliced thin
1 teaspoon fine sea salt, divided
No-Knead Pan Pizza Dough (page 32)
Freshly ground black pepper

1 Preheat the oven to 500°F.

2 In a medium bowl, whisk together the crème fraîche, fromage blanc, White Sauce, and nutmeg until well blended.

3 In a large skillet over medium heat, cook the bacon, stirring occasionally, until lightly crisp, about 6 minutes. Using a slotted spoon, transfer the bacon to a paper towel–lined plate.

4 Add the onion to the skillet. Season with ½ teaspoon of salt and cook, stirring frequently, until translucent, about 5 minutes. The onions shouldn't take color but should be soft. Using a slotted spoon, transfer the cooked onion to a fine-mesh strainer and gently press out any excess fat.

5 Leaving a 1-inch border, spread the cheese mixture in a thin layer over the dough. Top with an even layer of onions and scatter on the bacon.

6 Transfer the pizza to the oven and bake until the crust is deeply golden, 8 to 10 minutes.

7 Remove the pizza from the oven and let it rest for 5 minutes, then season with the remaining $\frac{1}{2}$ teaspoon of salt, and pepper. Slice and serve.

Cooking with kids: *Ask the kids to develop their arm strength by thoroughly blending the cheeses with a wooden spoon, and then, as the mixture softens, a whisk.*

Prosciutto & Arugula Pizza

MAKES 2 (12- TO 14-INCH) PIZZAS OR 4 PERSONAL PIZZAS

Prosciutto and arugula are delicious, classically Italian pizza toppings. This is a favorite in our house, and a great way to sneak some greens into the family's meal.

PREP TIME: 10 minutes
COOK TIME: 20 minutes
TOTAL TIME: 35 minutes

Cornmeal or flour, for dusting

2 tablespoons extra-virgin olive oil, plus more for brushing

Simply Amazing Pizza Dough (page 25) or Pro Dough (page 27)

1 cup New York–Style Pizza Sauce (page 40)

8 slices prosciutto

6 ounces fresh mozzarella cheese, sliced or shredded

3 cups arugula

¼ teaspoon salt

⅛ teaspoon freshly ground black pepper

3 ounces Parmesan cheese, shaved with a vegetable peeler

1 Preheat the oven and pizza stone (if using) to 500°F. Dust a pizza peel with cornmeal (if using a pizza stone), or brush two baking sheets with olive oil.

2 Roll out one of the dough balls to the desired size, and place it on the pizza peel (if using a pizza stone) or on the prepared baking sheet.

3 Leaving a 1-inch border, spread half of the sauce evenly onto the dough. Lay half of the prosciutto slices on top, then finish with half of the mozzarella.

4 Transfer the pizza to the hot pizza stone or oven rack, and bake until the crust is golden and the cheese has melted, 5 to 7 minutes on the pizza stone or 7 to 10 minutes on the baking sheet.

5 Remove the pizza from the oven and transfer it to a cutting board. Let it rest for 5 minutes, then top with half of the arugula, olive oil, salt, pepper, and Parmesan. Slice and serve.

6 Repeat with the remaining dough ball and toppings.

COOKING TIP: *Rinse and spin the arugula in advance, allowing it to dry completely before storing and refrigerating in resealable bags. Still-damp arugula makes for a soggy pie.*

Pancetta, Egg & Spinach Pizza

MAKES 2 (12- TO 14-INCH) PIZZAS OR 4 PERSONAL PIZZAS

This is my favorite brunch pizza. As a runner, I spend Sunday mornings running my longest distance of the week, after which a refueling meal isn't only welcome but necessary. This pizza, with the protein of a sunny side–up egg and a healthy serving of spinach, is not only a nutritionally sound post-run meal, it's so incredibly delicious that, around mile 9 or 10, it keeps me motivated toward the finish line. #Rungry

PREP TIME: 10 minutes
COOK TIME: 30 minutes
TOTAL TIME: 45 minutes

Cornmeal or flour, for dusting

1 tablespoon extra-virgin olive oil,
   plus more for brushing

3 ounces pancetta, finely diced

2 garlic cloves, minced

4 cups baby spinach, stems removed

¼ teaspoon salt

Simply Amazing Pizza Dough (page 25)
   or Pro Dough (page 27)

1 cup New York–Style Pizza Sauce (page 40)

1 cup grated fontina cheese

2 large eggs

2 tablespoons grated Parmesan cheese

2 tablespoons chopped fresh flat-leaf parsley

⅛ teaspoon freshly ground black pepper

1 Preheat the oven and pizza stone (if using) to 500°F. Dust a pizza peel with cornmeal (if using a pizza stone), or brush two baking sheets with olive oil.

2 In a large skillet over medium heat, cook the pancetta until crisp, about 5 minutes, turning frequently. Transfer to a paper towel–lined plate.

3 Discard the rendered fat from the skillet and add the olive oil. Return the skillet to medium heat and, when the oil begins to shimmer, add the garlic. Swirl the garlic in the pan for a minute, then add the spinach. Use tongs to turn the spinach, watching it decrease in volume. Cook the spinach for 2 to 3 minutes, until it's wilted but still has structure. Season with the salt and remove the skillet from the heat. Roughly chop the spinach. ➤

4 Roll out one of the dough balls to the desired size, and place it on the pizza peel (if using a pizza stone) or on the prepared baking sheet.

5 Leaving a 1-inch border, spread the sauce evenly onto the dough.

6 Top with half of the fontina followed by half of the spinach. Crack one egg, positioning the yolk in the center of the pizza. (If using a pizza peel, I find it easier to transfer the pizza to the oven, pull the oven rack out, and then crack the egg over the top.) Sprinkle with half of the Parmesan.

7 Transfer the pizza to the hot pizza stone or oven rack, and bake until the crust is golden and the egg yolk holds its shape when jiggled, 5 to 7 minutes on the pizza stone or 7 to 10 minutes on the baking sheet.

8 Remove the pizza from the oven and transfer it to a cutting board. Let it rest for 5 minutes, then season with half of the parsley and black pepper. Slice and serve.

9 Repeat from step 4 with the remaining dough ball and toppings.

A CLOSER LOOK: *Pancetta is salted, cured pork belly. It's often called Italian bacon, but pancetta is not smoked and is sold thinly sliced from round slabs.*

Chicken, Kale & Butternut Squash Pizza

MAKES 2 (12- TO 14-INCH) PIZZAS OR 4 PERSONAL PIZZAS

Serve this when you want your pizza to have more of a full meal balance of protein and vegetables. The flavors of Gruyère and Asiago are substantial enough to stand up to the rest of the ingredients. Rotisserie chicken—purchased from the grocery store—comes to the rescue when you're short on time, but this pizza also makes perfect use of leftover chicken.

PREP TIME: 10 minutes
COOK TIME: 40 minutes
TOTAL TIME: 55 minutes

Cornmeal or flour, for dusting

3 tablespoons extra-virgin olive oil, divided, plus more for brushing and drizzling

2 cups diced butternut squash

1 fresh rosemary sprig, stemmed and chopped

Salt

Freshly ground black pepper

3 cups stemmed, roughly chopped kale

1½ cups shredded cooked chicken

Simply Amazing Pizza Dough (page 25)

1½ cups grated Gruyère cheese

3 tablespoons grated Asiago cheese

2 tablespoons toasted walnuts, roughly chopped (see page 150 for toasting walnuts)

1 Preheat the oven and pizza stone (if using) to 500°F. Dust a pizza peel with cornmeal (if using a pizza stone), or brush two baking sheets with olive oil.

2 In a medium skillet over medium-high heat, heat 1 tablespoon of olive oil. When it shimmers, add the butternut squash and rosemary. Season with salt and pepper. Cook the squash until tender and browned, about 20 minutes, stirring frequently.

3 In a large bowl, use your hands to toss the kale and shredded chicken with the remaining 2 tablespoons of olive oil, and season with salt and pepper.

4 Roll out one of the dough balls to the desired size, and place it on the pizza peel (if using a pizza stone) or on the prepared baking sheet. ➤

5 Sprinkle half of the Gruyère over the dough and top with half of the kale and chicken, followed by half of the caramelized butternut squash and Asiago.

6 Transfer the pizza to the hot pizza stone or oven rack, and bake until the crust is golden and the cheese has melted, 5 to 7 minutes on the pizza stone or 7 to 10 minutes on the baking sheet.

7 Remove the pizza from the oven and transfer it to a cutting board. Let it rest for 5 minutes, then drizzle it with a little olive oil, season with salt and pepper, and sprinkle on half of the walnuts. Slice and serve.

8 Repeat from step 4 with the remaining dough ball and toppings.

COOKING TIP: *The butternut squash can be sautéed the night before and refrigerated overnight.*

Chicken, Pesto & Ricotta Pizza

MAKES 2 (12- TO 14-INCH) PIZZAS OR 4 PERSONAL PIZZAS

Bright garden flavors give leftover rotisserie chicken a fresh face, and the combination of ricotta and pesto is a creamy, wonderfully fragrant crowd pleaser. Add a few slices of prosciutto to the finished pizza for a sweet/salty edge.

PREP TIME: 10 minutes
COOK TIME: 20 minutes
TOTAL TIME: 35 minutes

Cornmeal or flour, for dusting

2 tablespoons extra-virgin olive oil, plus more for brushing

Simply Amazing Pizza Dough (page 25) or Pro Dough (page 27)

2 cups whole-milk ricotta cheese

1 cup Basil Pesto (page 44)

2 cups shredded cooked chicken

2 plum tomatoes, sliced thin

¼ cup freshly grated pecorino romano cheese

⅛ teaspoon freshly ground black pepper, plus more for finishing

1 Preheat the oven and pizza stone (if using) to 500°F. Dust a pizza peel with cornmeal (if using a pizza stone), or brush two baking sheets with olive oil.

2 Roll out one of the dough balls to the desired size, and place it on the pizza peel (if using a pizza stone) or on the prepared baking sheet.

3 Spoon half of the ricotta in dollops onto the dough and spread it into a thin, even layer. Spoon half of the Basil Pesto on top of the ricotta, spread it out, and sprinkle on half of the shredded chicken and tomato slices. Drizzle with half of the olive oil, sprinkle with half of the pecorino romano, and season with half of the black pepper.

4 Transfer the pizza to the hot pizza stone or oven rack, and bake until the crust is golden and the cheese has melted, 5 to 7 minutes on the pizza stone or 7 to 10 minutes on the baking sheet. ➤

5 Remove the pizza from the oven and transfer it to a cutting board. Let it rest for 5 minutes, then season with another grind or two of black pepper. Slice and serve.

6 Repeat with the remaining dough ball and toppings.

A CLOSER LOOK: *Pecorino romano is a hard, aged sheep's milk cheese with a pronounced saltiness. It goes everywhere Parmesan does (grated for pastas, pizza, and salads) but costs less.*

Grilled Clam & Corn Pizza

MAKES 2 (12- TO 14-INCH) PIZZAS OR 4 PERSONAL PIZZAS

Make this pizza in the summertime when corn is at its best. Littleneck clams, small as their name suggests, are the best size clam to use. If cherry stones are the only game in town, chop them after steaming.

PREP TIME: 15 minutes
COOK TIME: 30 minutes
TOTAL TIME: 45 minutes

6 ears corn, shucked

1 tablespoon extra-virgin olive oil, plus more for drizzling

2 dozen littleneck clams, scrubbed

Simply Amazing Pizza Dough (page 25) or Pro Dough (page 27)

2 pinches red pepper flakes

3 tablespoons chopped fresh flat-leaf parsley

1 Preheat a grill to indirect high heat (see page 14 for instructions) or a grill pan to high heat.

2 Rub the corn with the olive oil and grill over direct high heat for 5 minutes, turning every minute or two, until lightly charred on all sides. Remove the corn from the heat and cut the kernels from the cobs into a large bowl.

3 In a large pot with a lid, bring 1 inch of water to a boil over high heat. Add the clams, cover, and cook for 3 to 5 minutes, or until the clams open. Loosen the clams from their shells, and transfer to a medium bowl. Discard the shells and any clams that did not open.

4 Roll out one of the dough balls to the desired size.

5 Grill the dough on each side for 2 to 3 minutes (see page 14 for grilling pizza dough), remove from the heat, and top with half of the grilled corn and steamed clams. Season with a pinch of red pepper flakes and a drizzle of olive oil. Return the pizza to the grill, cover, and grill until the crust is well browned, about 5 minutes.

6 Transfer to a cutting board and sprinkle with half of the chopped parsley. Slice and serve.

7 Repeat from step 4 with the remaining dough ball and toppings.

PREP TIP: *The corn can be grilled a day in advance or, cut from the cob and sautéed with a little olive and salt. Refrigerate, covered, for up to 2 days.*

Seasonal Spotlight: Fall

Fall is the intersection of the last of the late summer fruits and vegetables and a whole new crop of deeper, earthier flavors at a time of year when everyone starts to crave heartier meals. Combine still-tender greens with autumn pumpkin, squashes, and even pears and apples for seasonally driven pizzas that are as beautiful as they are tasty. Root vegetables, mushrooms, and broccoli together with the last of the tomatoes are a way of holding on to the wonderful warmth of summer with great enthusiasm for the season ahead.

Fig, Prosciutto & Goat Cheese Pizza

MAKES 2 (12- TO 14-INCH) PIZZAS OR 4 PERSONAL PIZZAS

PREP TIME: 10 minutes
COOK TIME: 20 minutes
TOTAL TIME: 35 minutes

Cornmeal or flour, for dusting

2 tablespoons extra-virgin olive oil, plus more for brushing

Simply Amazing Pizza Dough (page 25) or Pro Dough (page 27)

¼ cup fig jam

½ cup shredded mozzarella cheese

½ cup crumbled goat cheese

8 slices prosciutto

8 figs, stemmed and quartered

4 fresh thyme sprigs, stemmed

¼ teaspoon fine sea salt

⅛ teaspoon freshly ground black pepper

1 Preheat the oven and pizza stone (if using) to 500°F. Dust a pizza peel with cornmeal (if using a pizza stone), or brush two baking sheets with olive oil.

2 Roll out one of the dough balls to the desired size, and place it on the pizza peel (if using a pizza stone) or on the prepared baking sheet.

3 Leaving a 1-inch border, spoon half of the fig jam evenly onto the dough. Top with half of the mozzarella, goat cheese, and prosciutto. Arrange half of the figs on the pizza, sprinkle on half of the thyme, and season with half of the salt and pepper.

4 Transfer the pizza to the hot pizza stone or oven rack, and bake until the crust is golden and the cheese has melted, 5 to 7 minutes on the pizza stone or 7 to 10 minutes on the baking sheet.

5 Remove the pizza from the oven and transfer it to a cutting board. Let it rest for 5 minutes, then drizzle with half of the olive oil. Slice and serve.

6 Repeat with the remaining dough ball and toppings.

 Adventurous addition: *Instead of goat cheese, try using Gorgonzola for an earthy, blue-veined unctuousness. With either cheese, top the pizza with a small handful of arugula leaves after cooking.*

VEGAN & VEGETARIAN

6

The meat-free zone is an exciting one for pizza and the people who love it. After all, pizza is an ideal showcase for vegetables. Throughout Italy, regional flatbreads and pizza will feature one topping—mushrooms or fennel, for instance—without sauce, cheese, or any adornment other than salt and olive oil. Reverence for the ingredients is what it's all about.

And then there're the people. For vegetarians and vegans, pizza is the social food, allowing for group dinners with options for all. The recipes in this chapter are vegetable focused with an eye toward gluten-free and dairy-free eating.

To me, pizza is in many ways an extension of salad: If I like it in a bowl, I'll love it warm on a pizza. This rings especially true as a parent, when the perpetual goal of pumping veggies into kids is best achieved using the slice: Broccoli rabe chopped nearly to a pesto and scattered over sauce is impossible for any kid to eradicate. It's an old trick, but it still works—deliciously so.

Ricotta Margherita

MAKES 2 (12- TO 14-INCH) PIZZAS OR 4 PERSONAL PIZZAS

As recognizable as the Italian flag, tomato sauce and milky fresh cheese are emblematic of the transcendent simplicity of pizza. This version, with ricotta and cherry tomatoes, layers a bit more texture on to the classic and maximizes the flavors.

▼

NUT-FREE

▼

VEGETARIAN

PREP TIME: 10 minutes
COOK TIME: 20 minutes
TOTAL TIME: 35 minutes

Cornmeal or flour, for dusting

1 tablespoon extra-virgin olive oil, plus more for brushing

Simply Amazing Pizza Dough (page 25) or Pro Dough (page 27)

1 cup New York–Style Pizza Sauce (page 40)

1 teaspoon dried oregano

½ cup fresh ricotta cheese

6 ounces fresh mozzarella cheese, sliced thin

¼ teaspoon fine sea salt

⅛ teaspoon freshly ground black pepper

8 fresh basil leaves, torn

1 Preheat the oven and pizza stone (if using) to 500°F. Dust a pizza peel with cornmeal (if using a pizza stone), or brush two baking sheets with olive oil.

2 Roll out one of the dough balls to the desired size, and place it on the pizza peel (if using a pizza stone) or on the prepared baking sheet.

3 Leaving a 1-inch border, spoon half of the sauce onto the dough, spreading it evenly. Sprinkle on half of the oregano.

4 Spoon half of the ricotta cheese in small dollops all over the pizza, then arrange half of the mozzarella slices on top. Season with half of the salt and pepper, and scatter on half of the torn basil leaves.

5 Transfer the pizza to the hot pizza stone or oven rack, and bake until the crust is golden and the cheese has melted, 5 to 7 minutes on the pizza stone or 7 to 10 minutes on the baking sheet.

6 Remove the pizza from the oven and transfer it to a cutting board. Let it rest for 5 minutes. Slice and serve.

7 Repeat with the remaining dough ball and toppings.

Cooking with kids: *Pizza, either hand stretched or rolled with a pin, is rustic food, often irregularly shaped and prized for its handmade appearance. As kids develop a feel for working with dough, they might pursue a symmetrical pie or they might not. That, I find, is personality driven.*

Vegan Spinach & Mushroom Pizza

MAKES 2 (12- TO 14-INCH) PIZZAS OR 4 PERSONAL PIZZAS

If I'm making a vegan pizza, I'm happy to skip the cheese entirely, as vegetable toppings can be fully magnificent on their own. For others, the need for cheese can run deep. This pizza joins the melt of vegan mozzarella and the taste and texture of Cashew Cheese for the best of both worlds: meltability and a rich, fat-filled flavor. The onions go on raw, charring in the oven to provide a little peppery bite.

PREP TIME: 15 minutes
COOK TIME: 30 minutes
TOTAL TIME: 50 minutes

Cornmeal or flour, for dusting

4 tablespoons extra-virgin olive oil, divided, plus more for brushing

2 cups sliced cremini mushrooms

½ teaspoon fine sea salt

1 garlic clove, minced

⅛ teaspoon red pepper flakes

4 cups baby spinach, stems removed

Simply Amazing Pizza Dough (page 25) or Pro Dough (page 27)

1 cup New York–Style Pizza Sauce (page 40)

½ cup grated vegan mozzarella or Cheddar cheese

½ cup Cashew Cheese (page 43) or other nut-based non-dairy cheese

¼ cup sliced black olives

½ medium yellow onion, sliced thin

1 Preheat the oven and pizza stone (if using) to 500°F. Dust a pizza peel with cornmeal (if using a pizza stone), or brush two baking sheets with olive oil.

2 In a large skillet over medium-high heat, heat 3 tablespoons of olive oil until it shimmers. Add the mushrooms and salt, and let the mushrooms sit undisturbed for 2 minutes. Give the pan a shake and continue cooking for 3 minutes more, stirring occasionally, until the mushrooms have taken color but are still firm and vibrant. Using a slotted spoon, transfer the mushrooms to a medium bowl.

3 Reduce the heat to medium, add the remaining 1 tablespoon of olive oil to the skillet, then add the garlic and red pepper flakes. Swirl the skillet to flavor the oil, then add the spinach. Use tongs to turn the spinach, watching it decrease in

volume. Cook the spinach for 2 to 3 minutes, until it's wilted but still has structure. Remove the skillet from the heat.

4 Roll out one of the dough balls to the desired size, and place it on the pizza peel (if using a pizza stone) or on the prepared baking sheet.

5 Leaving a 1-inch border, spoon half of the sauce onto the dough, spreading it evenly. Top with half of the vegan mozzarella and Cashew Cheese. Scatter half of the spinach and mushrooms over the pizza, followed by half of the black olives and sliced onion.

6 Transfer the pizza to the hot pizza stone or oven rack, and bake until the crust is golden and the cheese has melted, 5 to 7 minutes on the pizza stone or 7 to 10 minutes on the baking sheet.

7 Remove the pizza from the oven and transfer it to a cutting board. Let it rest for 5 minutes. Slice and serve.

8 Repeat with the remaining dough ball and toppings.

Cooking with kids: *With slightly more than the usual amount of pizza ingredients, this pie is a great opportunity to have the kids arrange the assembly line of ingredients for stress-free prep, using a bowl for each ingredient.*

Garden Pan Pizza

MAKES 1 PAN PIZZA

I use oven-roasted vegetables from breakfast to dinner. They can be made ahead of time and then refrigerated, ready to go anywhere from grain salads to soup purées. As a pizza topping, they're deeply flavorful, textured, and hearty—an easy midweek dinner requiring next to no effort.

PREP TIME: 15 minutes
COOK TIME: 45 minutes
TOTAL TIME: 1 hour, 5 minutes

2 red bell peppers, cut into strips

1 zucchini, trimmed and cut into ¼-inch rounds

1 yellow summer squash, trimmed and cut into ¼-inch rounds

1 medium red onion, sliced

10 ounces fingerling or red bliss potatoes, scrubbed and cut into ¼-inch slices

3 tablespoons extra-virgin olive oil

5 fresh thyme sprigs, stemmed

½ teaspoon fine sea salt

¼ teaspoon freshly ground black pepper

1 cup New York–Style Pizza Sauce (page 40)

No-Knead Pan Pizza Dough (page 32)

1¼ cups grated fontina cheese

1½ cups arugula

1 Preheat the oven to 450°F.

2 On a foil-lined baking tray, spread the bell peppers, zucchini, summer squash, onion, and potatoes. Drizzle with the olive oil, sprinkle on the thyme, and season with the salt and pepper. Toss well, then transfer the baking sheet to the oven and roast for about 30 minutes, stirring twice during cooking. The potatoes should be fork tender.

3 Remove the vegetables from the oven and set aside. At this point, they can be used immediately or cooled to room temperature and refrigerated overnight in an airtight container.

4 Raise the oven temperature to 500°F.

5 Leaving a 1-inch border, spoon the sauce onto the dough, spreading it evenly. Scatter the fontina cheese over the dough, followed by the roasted vegetables.

6 Bake the pizza until the cheese has melted and the crust is golden, about 15 minutes. Remove it from the oven and let it cool for 5 minutes, then top it with the fresh arugula. Slice and serve.

Cooking with kids: *Let your kids build the recipe by picking their three favorite vegetables for this pizza: carrots, broccoli, butternut squash, or parsnips would all be good candidates. Peppers and onions should remain to add sweetness and color.*

Roasted Cauliflower, Fontina & Mushroom Pizza

MAKES 1 (12- TO 14-INCH) PIZZA OR 2 PERSONAL PIZZAS

This pizza makes the most of the versatility of cauliflower, featuring it in the dough as well as in the topping. Fontina and mushrooms are wonderful together, but use Cashew Cheese (page 43) if a vegan pizza is what you're after.

GLUTEN-FREE

NUT-FREE

VEGETARIAN

PREP TIME: 10 minutes
COOK TIME: 45 minutes
TOTAL TIME: 1 hour

3½ tablespoons extra-virgin olive oil, divided, plus more for greasing
½ head cauliflower, cut into bite-size florets
½ teaspoon salt, divided
¼ teaspoon freshly ground black pepper, divided
3 cups assorted mushrooms (about 12 ounces), stemmed and cut into ¼-inch-thick slices
3 fresh thyme sprigs, stemmed
Cauliflower Pizza Dough (page 33)
½ cup No-Cook Pizza Sauce (page 41)
½ cup crumbled fontina cheese
1 fresh oregano sprig, stemmed

1 Preheat the oven to 450°F. Coat a baking sheet lightly with olive oil.

2 Spread the cauliflower on a second baking sheet, drizzle with 1½ tablespoons of olive oil, and toss by hand. Season with half of the salt and pepper. Transfer the baking sheet to the oven and roast the cauliflower until tender and lightly browned, about 20 minutes, stirring midway through. Remove from the oven and set aside to cool.

3 Meanwhile, in a large skillet over medium-high heat, heat the remaining 2 tablespoons of olive oil. Add the mushrooms, season with the thyme and remaining ¼ teaspoon of salt, and let the mushrooms sit undisturbed for 2 minutes. Give the pan a shake and continue cooking for 3 minutes more, stirring occasionally, until the mushrooms have taken color but are still firm and vibrant. Season with the remaining ⅛ teaspoon of pepper and, using a slotted spoon, transfer the mushrooms to a plate.

4 Pat the Cauliflower Pizza Dough onto the prepared baking sheet. Transfer the sheet to the oven and bake the dough for 15 minutes, or until it begins to crisp at the edges. Remove the crust from the oven.

5 Leaving a 1-inch border, spoon the sauce onto the crust, spreading it evenly. Top with the fontina, roasted cauliflower, and sautéed mushrooms. Return the pizza to the oven and cook for 4 to 5 minutes, or until the cheese is melted and the crust is golden.

6 Remove the pizza from the oven and transfer it to a cutting board. Garnish with the oregano and let it rest for 5 minutes. Slice and serve.

Cooking with kids: *Mushrooms can be easily sliced with a paring knife, the perfect-size knife for small hands.*

Potato, Pesto & Garlic Pizza

MAKES 2 (12- TO 14-INCH) PIZZAS OR 4 PERSONAL PIZZAS

Potato-topped pizza, with nothing but olive oil and rosemary to adorn it, is common in Italy. It travels well at room temperature and makes a handy lunch on the road, but this dressed-up version is especially delicious hot out of the oven.

PREP TIME: 10 minutes
COOK TIME: 45 minutes
TOTAL TIME: 1 hour

Cornmeal or flour, for dusting

3 tablespoons extra-virgin olive oil, plus more for brushing and drizzling

6 medium Yukon gold potatoes, scrubbed

1 fresh rosemary sprig, stemmed

Simply Amazing Pizza Dough (page 25) or Pro Dough (page 27)

1 cup Basil Pesto (page 44)

¼ teaspoon salt

⅛ teaspoon freshly ground black pepper

4 to 6 cloves Balsamic-Roasted Garlic (page 46), mashed

1 Preheat the oven and pizza stone (if using) to 500°F. Dust a pizza peel with cornmeal (if using a pizza stone), or brush two baking sheets with olive oil.

2 In a heavy, ovenproof skillet, heat the oil. When it shimmers, add the potatoes and the rosemary. Cook until the potatoes are lightly browned on all sides, about 8 minutes total. Transfer the skillet to the oven and cook until the potatoes are tender but still hold their shape, about 15 minutes. Remove the skillet from the oven and set it aside to cool. When the potatoes are cool enough to handle, cut them into ½-inch slices.

3 Roll out one of the dough balls to the desired size, and place it on the pizza peel (if using a pizza stone) or on the prepared baking sheet.

4 Leaving a 1-inch border, spoon half of the Basil Pesto onto the dough, spreading it evenly. Top the pizza with half of the potato slices. Drizzle with a little olive oil and season with half of the salt and pepper.

5 Transfer the pizza to the hot pizza stone or oven rack, and bake until the crust is golden, 5 to 7 minutes on the pizza stone or 7 to 10 minutes on the baking sheet.

6 Remove the pizza from the oven and transfer it to a cutting board. Let it rest for 5 minutes, then spread half of the Balsamic-Roasted Garlic over the pizza. Slice and serve.

7 Repeat from step 3 with the remaining dough ball and toppings.

PREP TIP: *The potatoes can be cooked in advance, but keep them whole to avoid drying out. Slice just before using.*

Rosemary & Pear Pizza

MAKES 1 (12- TO 14-INCH) PIZZA

Fruit pizzas are common in southern Italy, and this one, on the sweet side, is what I think of as a brunch pizza. Great with coffee or prosecco, it's a surprising and somewhat elegant way to serve fall fruit.

▼

NUT-FREE

▼

VEGAN

PREP TIME: 15 minutes
COOK TIME: 20 minutes
TOTAL TIME: 40 minutes

½ recipe Simply Amazing
    Pizza Dough (page 25)
4 Bosc pears
½ lemon
Zest of 1 orange
1 tablespoon chopped fresh basil leaves
1 teaspoon chopped fresh rosemary leaves
2 tablespoons sugar
⅛ teaspoon freshly ground black pepper
2 tablespoons extra-virgin olive oil

1 Preheat the oven and pizza stone (if using) to 450°F.

2 On a baking sheet, roll out the pizza dough to form a 12- to 14-inch disc.

3 Peel, halve, and cut away the core of the pears. Slice each pear half into thin wedges. Squeeze lemon juice over the pears.

4 Arrange the pears, starting at the outer edge of the crust (leaving no border), in a spiral toward the center. Sprinkle the orange zest, basil, rosemary, sugar, and pepper over the pears. Drizzle with the olive oil.

5 Bake for 20 minutes, until the pizza appears golden and crisp.

6 Remove the pizza from the oven and let sit for 5 minutes. Slice and serve warm or at room temperature.

 **Cooking with kids:** *Geometry lessons ensue here. Arranging the pears is the time to teach kids about concentric circles.*

Roasted Eggplant, Smoked Mozzarella & Cherry Tomato Pizza

MAKES 2 (12- TO 14-INCH) PIZZAS OR 4 PERSONAL PIZZAS

Smoked mozzarella adds depth to this simple flavor combination of eggplant and tomato. Eggplant is one of the tastiest pizza toppings, but not always one of the prettiest. Seek out multi-toned cherry tomatoes to dress up this pizza.

NUT-FREE

VEGETARIAN

PREP TIME: 10 minutes, plus 10 minutes to sit
COOK TIME: 30 minutes
TOTAL TIME: 50 minutes

Cornmeal or flour, for dusting

Simply Amazing Pizza Dough (page 25)

½ teaspoon salt

1 large eggplant, peeled and cut crosswise into ½-inch-thick slices

¼ cup extra-virgin olive oil, divided

6 ounces smoked mozzarella cheese, cut into ½-inch dice

14 cherry tomatoes, halved

1 tablespoon fresh oregano leaves, roughly chopped

¼ teaspoon fine sea salt

⅛ teaspoon freshly ground black pepper

1 Preheat a grill to indirect high heat (see page 14 for grilling instructions) or a grill pan on the stove to high heat. Dust a pizza peel with cornmeal.

2 Roll out one of the dough balls to the desired size and place it on the pizza peel.

3 Salt both sides of the eggplant slices and place them on a metal rack set over a rimmed baking sheet. Let sit for 10 minutes to draw the moisture out. Pat the slices dry with a paper towel and brush them lightly with 3 tablespoons of olive oil.

4 Grill the eggplant slices until tender, 5 to 6 minutes per side. The grill should be hot enough to char the eggplant. Transfer the grilled eggplant slices to a cutting board and cut into a rough dice. ➤

5 Grill the pizza dough on one side for 3 minutes, flip the dough, and then top the pizza with half of the eggplant, mozzarella, and tomatoes. Close the lid and grill the pizza until the crust is golden and the mozzarella has melted, about 7 minutes.

6 Transfer the pizza to a cutting board. Drizzle with half of the remaining olive oil and season with half of the oregano, sea salt, and pepper. Slice and serve.

7 Repeat with the remaining dough ball and toppings, skipping steps 3 and 4.

A CLOSER LOOK: *Look for smooth, wrinkle-free eggplants with vibrant green stems. Smaller Italian eggplants are preferable to the larger, more bitter and heavily seeded variety. Japanese eggplants, longer and thinner, have a creamy texture that, while delicious, can be tricky with pizza.*

Chipotle–Black Bean Pizza

MAKES 2 (12- TO 14-INCH) PIZZAS OR 4 PERSONAL PIZZAS

Both comforting and healthy, this vegan pizza has a protein-packed base of black beans enlivened with the color and crunch of avocado and bell pepper. A refreshing salad of crisp romaine dressed with olive oil and lemon would round this meal out nicely.

PREP TIME: 15 minutes
COOK TIME: 30 minutes
TOTAL TIME: 50 minutes

Cornmeal or flour, for dusting

2 tablespoons extra-virgin olive oil, plus more for brushing

¼ teaspoon dried oregano

1 medium yellow onion, diced

½ teaspoon salt, plus more for seasoning

2 garlic cloves

⅛ teaspoon freshly ground black pepper, plus more for seasoning

¼ cup low-sodium vegetable broth

2 cups canned black beans, rinsed

2 chipotle chiles in adobo, chopped, plus 1 tablespoon of the adobo sauce

Simply Amazing Pizza Dough (page 25)

1 cup grated vegan mozzarella cheese

1 red bell pepper, diced

1 cup diced avocado

½ cup fresh cilantro leaves

1 Preheat the oven and pizza stone (if using) to 500°F. Dust a pizza peel with cornmeal (if using a pizza stone), or brush two baking sheets with olive oil.

2 In a large skillet over medium-high heat, heat the olive oil and oregano. When it shimmers, add the diced onion and salt and cook, stirring occasionally, until the onions are soft and translucent, about 5 minutes. Add the garlic and cook 1 minute more, stirring to combine. Season with salt and add the pepper. Transfer to a small bowl.

3 Add the vegetable broth to the sauté pan, then add the black beans, chipotle chiles, and reserved adobo sauce. Bring to a simmer and begin to mash the beans using a potato masher or immersion blender until they form a rough paste (add more vegetable broth if necessary). Season with salt and pepper. Remove from the heat and set aside. ➤

4 Roll out one of the dough balls to the desired size, and place it on the pizza peel (if using a pizza stone) or on the prepared baking sheet.

5 Leaving a 1-inch border, spoon half of the black beans onto the crust, spreading them evenly. Top with half of the mozzarella and red pepper.

6 Transfer the pizza to the hot pizza stone or oven rack, and bake until the crust is golden and the cheese has melted, 5 to 7 minutes on the pizza stone or 7 to 10 minutes on the baking sheet.

7 Remove the pizza from the oven, transfer it to a cutting board, and let it sit for 5 minutes. Top the pizza with half of the avocado, cilantro, and freshly ground black pepper. Slice and serve.

8 Repeat from step 3 with the remaining dough ball and toppings.

Adventurous addition: *A roasted tomatillo salsa (either store-bought or homemade) adds a bright acidic edge to this pizza. Spoon it onto slices just before serving.*

Mediterranean Pizza

MAKES 2 (12- TO 14-INCH) PIZZAS OR 4 PERSONAL PIZZAS

With the trademark and well-loved flavors of a Greek salad, this lively pizza is filling and fragrant. Though it breaks the general pizza rule of no more than three toppings at once, these flavors are established friends that play well together.

PREP TIME: 10 minutes
COOK TIME: 30 minutes
TOTAL TIME: 45 minutes

Cornmeal or flour, for dusting
3 tablespoons extra-virgin olive oil, plus more for brushing
1 small red onion, diced (½ cup)
¼ teaspoon salt
⅛ teaspoon freshly ground black pepper
3 garlic cloves, minced
4 cups spinach, stems removed
¾ cup chopped fresh mint
Whole-Wheat Pizza Dough (page 29)
8 ounces crumbled feta cheese
½ cup halved black olives, preferably Kalamata
½ teaspoon dried oregano

1 Preheat the oven and pizza stone (if using) to 500°F. Dust a pizza peel with cornmeal (if using a pizza stone), or brush two baking sheets with olive oil.

2 In a large skillet over medium-high heat, heat the olive oil until it shimmers. Add the onions, season with the salt and pepper and cook until translucent, about 4 minutes. Lower the heat to medium and add the garlic. Cook until it's fragrant, about a minute more.

3 Add the spinach to the pan and use tongs to toss the leaves as they decrease in volume, about 4 minutes. Remove the pan from the heat and add the chopped mint.

4 Roll out one of the dough balls to the desired size, and place it on the pizza peel (if using a pizza stone) or on the prepared baking sheet.

5 Top the dough with half of the spinach mixture, then dot with half of the feta and olives. ➤

6 Transfer the pizza to the hot pizza stone or oven rack, and bake until the crust is golden, 5 to 7 minutes on the pizza stone or 7 to 10 minutes on the baking sheet.

7 Remove the pizza from the oven and transfer it to a cutting board. Let it rest for 5 minutes, then top with half of the dried oregano; slice and serve.

8 Repeat from step 4 with the remaining dough ball and toppings.

Keep it simple: *There are those who love mint in savory food and those who do not (many children fall into the latter category). Instead of combining the mint with the sautéed spinach, serve it separately as a topping choice.*

Fennel & Fontina Pizza with Olive Tapenade

MAKES 2 (12- TO 14-INCH) PIZZAS OR 4 PERSONAL PIZZAS

Fennel is one of the vegetables I rely on in winter. Raw in salads and roasted with meats, I love its distinctive flavor, versatility, and sturdiness; it can roll around in the crisper drawer for a week or two and still keep its good looks. This pizza rarely appeals to kids, but I like it for its Provençal vibe, especially in the colder months when, pairing it with a glass of Bandol, I count the days until summer.

▼
NUT-FREE

▼
VEGETARIAN

PREP TIME: 10 minutes
COOK TIME: 35 minutes
TOTAL TIME: 50 minutes

Cornmeal or flour, for dusting
2 tablespoons extra-virgin olive oil, plus more for brushing
4 fennel bulbs, stems and fronds discarded
¼ teaspoon salt
⅛ teaspoon freshly ground black pepper
Simply Amazing Pizza Dough (page 25)
1 cup grated fontina cheese
¼ cup Black Olive Tapenade (page 45)
1 tablespoon fresh marjoram or thyme leaves

1 Preheat the oven and pizza stone (if using) to 500°F. Dust a pizza peel with cornmeal (if using a pizza stone), or brush two baking sheets with olive oil.

2 Cut the fennel bulbs into quarters, remove the cores, and cut each quarter into thin strips. Spread the strips on a sheet, drizzle lightly with the olive oil, and season with the salt and pepper. Roast for 15 minutes, until tender. Remove from the oven and set aside.

3 Roll out one of the dough balls to the desired size, and place it on the pizza peel (if using a pizza stone) or on the prepared baking sheet.

4 Sprinkle half of the fontina over the dough, and top with half of the roasted fennel. Spoon half of the Black Olive Tapenade in dollops over the surface of the pizza. ➤

5 Transfer the pizza to the hot pizza stone or oven rack, and bake until the crust is golden, 5 to 7 minutes on the pizza stone or 7 to 10 minutes on the baking sheet.

6 Remove the pizza from the oven and transfer it to a cutting board. Let it rest for 5 minutes, then scatter half of the marjoram the over top. Slice and serve.

7 Repeat from step 3 with the remaining dough ball and toppings.

PREP TIP: *For quicker prep, roast the fennel for this pizza the night before, and assemble everything at cocktail hour (or homework hour, depending on what kind of party you're having that night).*

Spring Pea Pizza with Ramps, Mint & Ricotta

MAKES 2 (12- TO 14-INCH) PIZZAS OR 4 PERSONAL PIZZAS

This classic spring combination is both rustic and elegant. Ramps (wild, foraged onions) arrive at the farmers' market sometime around March. Chefs get pretty pumped up about ramps, partly because of their unique flavor and partly because they're one of the few foods that haven't been cultivated to year-round availability, so there's a get-'em-while-you-can excitement. Peas, equally celebrated whether fresh in spring or frozen all year long, are a sweet counterpoint.

▼

NUT-FREE

▼

VEGETARIAN

PREP TIME: 10 minutes
COOK TIME: 25 minutes
TOTAL TIME: 40 minutes

Cornmeal or flour, for dusting

2 tablespoons extra-virgin olive oil, plus more for brushing

½ cup shelled fresh English peas (or frozen and thawed peas)

10 ramps

¼ teaspoon fine sea salt

Simply Amazing Pizza Dough (page 25) or Pro Dough (page 27)

¾ cup ricotta cheese

2 tablespoons chopped fresh mint

1 Preheat the oven and pizza stone (if using) to 500°F. Dust a pizza peel with cornmeal (if using a pizza stone), or brush two baking sheets with olive oil.

2 If using fresh peas, bring a large pot of salted water to a boil. Fill a large bowl with ice water. Blanch the peas for 1 minute then, using a slotted spoon, transfer them to the ice water. Drain and set aside.

3 Spread the ramps on a baking sheet, drizzle with the olive oil, and sprinkle with the salt. Roast for 5 minutes to wilt. Transfer to a cutting board and cut into thirds.

4 Roll out one of the dough balls to the desired size, and place it on the pizza peel (if using a pizza stone) or on the prepared baking sheet. ➤

5 Spoon half of the ricotta in dollops all over the dough. Scatter on half of the peas, ramps, and mint.

6 Transfer the pizza to the hot pizza stone or oven rack, and bake until the crust is golden, 5 to 7 minutes on the pizza stone or 7 to 10 minutes on the baking sheet.

7 Remove the pizza from the oven, transfer it to a cutting board, and let it sit for 5 minutes. Slice and serve.

8 Repeat from step 4 with the remaining dough ball and toppings.

A CLOSER LOOK: *Ramps are foraged, found mainly in the Northeast, and have a pleasantly pungent aroma. If they're not available, scallions and leeks, sliced lengthwise, would be wonderful with this pizza.*

Cooking with kids: *If using fresh peas, ask the kids to shell them and compare their taste before and after blanching. Snap peas or frozen and thawed peas can be used when fresh English peas aren't available.*

Zucchini & Pistachio Pizza

MAKES 2 (12- TO 14-INCH) PIZZAS OR 4 PERSONAL PIZZAS

This vegan pizza skips cheese and any of its stand-ins entirely, as many classic Italian pizzas and flatbreads do. It's a pure approach, an opportunity to appreciate the beauty and simplicity of the vegetables. But, if you're one of those folks for whom warm, melted cheese is the whole reason to eat pizza, a mix of vegan mozzarella and goat cheese would be the ticket.

PREP TIME: 15 minutes
COOK TIME: 30 minutes
TOTAL TIME: 50 minutes

Cornmeal or flour, for dusting
2 tablespoons extra-virgin olive oil, plus more for brushing
1 medium green zucchini, halved lengthwise and cut thinly into half-moons
1 medium yellow summer squash, halved lengthwise and cut thinly into half-moons
¼ teaspoon salt
Simply Amazing Pizza Dough (page 25)
1 medium red onion, sliced thin
1 teaspoon fresh thyme leaves
¼ teaspoon red pepper flakes
1 teaspoon freshly squeezed lemon juice
¼ cup shelled pistachios, toasted (see page 163)

1 Preheat the oven and pizza stone (if using) to 500°F. Dust a pizza peel with cornmeal (if using a pizza stone), or brush two baking sheets with olive oil.

2 In a large strainer set over a large bowl, toss the zucchini and summer squash well with the salt, and let it sit for about 5 minutes. Use a kitchen towel to press and squeeze the liquid from the squash mixture, removing as much moisture as possible.

3 Roll out one of the dough balls to the desired size, and place it on the pizza peel (if using a pizza stone) or on the prepared baking sheet.

4 In a large mixing bowl, toss together the drained squash mixture, onion, thyme, red pepper flakes, olive oil, and lemon juice. Arrange half of the vegetables on the dough. ➤

5 Transfer the pizza to the hot pizza stone or oven rack, and bake until the crust is golden and the cheese has melted, 7 to 10 minutes on the pizza stone or 12 to 15 minutes on the baking sheet.

6 Remove the pizza from the oven and transfer it to a cutting board. Let it rest for 5 minutes, then garnish with half of the toasted pistachios. Slice and serve.

7 Repeat from step 3 with the remaining dough ball and toppings.

Adventurous addition: *Gremolata is a tireless condiment, boosting the flavor of roasted meats, salad dressings, and pastas. Reinforce the flavors in this pizza by topping it with a gentle smear for an herbaceous finishing touch after the cooking process. To make gremolata, toss a handful of roughly chopped parsley leaves with a clove of minced garlic, the zest of 1 lemon, and a drizzle of olive oil.*

Escarole & Radicchio Pizza

MAKES 1 PAN PIZZA

I fell in love with escarole at Lupa, Mario Batali's casual restaurant in Greenwich Village. Since it opened, they've served a salad of escarole, red onion, walnuts, and pecorino. It's one of those combinations that's disarmingly simple but endlessly crave-worthy. The combination of the slightly bitter greens, peppery red onion, and mellow cheese makes for an equally tasty pizza that's deliciously satisfying and meat-free.

PREP TIME: 10 minutes
COOK TIME: 20 minutes
TOTAL TIME: 35 minutes

1 head escarole, cored, center ribs removed, leaves chopped
½ head radicchio, sliced
1 small red onion, sliced thin
1 tablespoon extra-virgin olive oil
¼ teaspoon fine sea salt
Pinch red pepper flakes
No-Knead Pan Pizza Dough (page 32)
6 slices provolone cheese
½ cup grated pecorino romano cheese
¼ cup walnuts, toasted (see page 150 for toasting walnuts)

1 Preheat the oven to 500°F.

2 Toss the escarole, radicchio, and red onion slices in a bowl with the olive oil. Season with the salt and red pepper flakes. Cover the dough with the slices of provolone. Top the pizza with the escarole mixture, spreading it into a thin, even layer. Sprinkle with the pecorino.

3 Transfer the pizza to the oven and bake until the crust is golden, about 20 minutes.

4 Remove the pizza from the oven and use a spatula to transfer it to a cutting board. Let it sit for 5 minutes. Top the pizza with a drizzle of olive oil and the toasted walnuts. Slice and serve.

Cooking with kids: *Greens, yielding and easy to cut, are a good way for kids to develop basic knife skills. Ask the kids to cut the radicchio and tear or cut the escarole into ½-inch strips (yes, the Type A's can use a ruler).*

Brussels Sprout, Mozzarella & Sage Pizza

MAKES 2 (12- TO 14-INCH) PIZZAS OR 4 PERSONAL PIZZAS

With kids, presentation can make all the difference. Brussels sprouts in their natural form can be a deal breaker for children who are convinced that they don't like vegetables. Those same Brussels sprouts, shredded into a more approachable slaw-like form, are often gobbled up. It's worth a try, especially when the result is a phenomenally delicious little pizza.

PREP TIME: 10 minutes
COOK TIME: 30 minutes
TOTAL TIME: 45 minutes

Cornmeal or flour, for dusting
2 tablespoons extra-virgin olive oil, plus more for brushing and drizzling
1 red onion, sliced
½ teaspoon fine sea salt, divided
⅛ teaspoon freshly ground black pepper
Simply Amazing Pizza Dough (page 25) or Pro Dough (page 27)
6 ounces fresh mozzarella cheese, shredded
12 Brussels sprouts, shredded or finely sliced
8 sage leaves, rolled and sliced thin
¼ cup grated Parmesan cheese
2 pinches red pepper flakes

1 Preheat the oven and pizza stone (if using) to 500°F. Dust a pizza peel with cornmeal (if using a pizza stone), or brush two baking sheets with olive oil.

2 Spread the onion on a sheet tray, drizzle with the olive oil, and toss to coat. Season with ¼ teaspoon of salt, and the pepper. Transfer the baking sheet to the oven and roast for 10 to 12 minutes, or until the onions are caramelized. Remove from the oven and set aside.

3 Roll out one of the dough balls to the desired size, and place it on the pizza peel (if using a pizza stone) or on the prepared baking sheet.

4 Top the dough with half of the mozzarella, Brussels sprouts, and roasted red onion. Sprinkle on the remaining ¼ teaspoon of salt, half of the sage, and half of the Parmesan, followed by a drizzle of olive oil and a pinch of red pepper flakes.

5 Transfer the pizza to the hot pizza stone or oven rack, and bake until the crust is golden and the cheese has melted, 5 to 7 minutes on the pizza stone or 7 to 10 minutes on the baking sheet.

6 Remove the pizza from the oven and transfer it to a cutting board. Let it rest for 5 minutes. Slice and serve.

7 Repeat from step 3 with the remaining dough ball and toppings.

COOKING TIP: *This recipe comes together quickly if you own an inexpensive Japanese mandoline called a Benriner (but remember, children and mandolines do not mix). If using a chef's knife, cut the sprouts in half, place the flat side on a cutting board, and cut into thin slices.*

Spinach & Gruyère Pizza with Chili Oil

MAKES 2 (12- TO 14-INCH) PIZZAS OR 4 PERSONAL PIZZAS

While some pizzas feature spinach as a supporting player, here it's the main event. The leaves go on raw and are wilted by the oven, giving them a roasted quality. The blend of cheeses along with Chili Oil makes this an ultra-savory, spicy pie that's surprisingly addictive.

PREP TIME: 15 minutes
COOK TIME: 20 minutes
TOTAL TIME: 40 minutes

Cornmeal or flour, for dusting, or extra-virgin olive oil, for brushing
Simply Amazing Pizza Dough (page 25)
2 garlic cloves, minced
½ cup grated pecorino romano cheese
¾ cup grated Gruyère cheese
¾ cup shredded fresh mozzarella cheese
5 cups baby spinach leaves, stems removed
¼ teaspoon fine sea salt
2 tablespoons Chili Oil (page 51)

1 Preheat the oven and pizza stone (if using) to 500°F. Dust a pizza peel with cornmeal (if using a pizza stone), or brush two baking sheets with olive oil.

2 Roll out one of the dough balls to the desired size, and place it on the pizza peel (if using a pizza stone) or on the prepared baking sheet.

3 Scatter half of the garlic over the dough and sprinkle with half of the pecorino, Gruyère, and mozzarella cheeses.

4 Transfer the pizza to the oven and bake just until the cheese melts, 2 to 3 minutes.

5 Remove the pizza from the oven, top it with half of the spinach and salt, and drizzle with 1 tablespoon of Chili Oil. Return the pizza to the oven and bake for another 4 to 5 minutes, or until the spinach wilts and begins to char.

6 Remove the pizza from the oven and transfer it to a cutting board. Let it rest for 5 minutes, then slice and serve.

7 Repeat with the remaining dough ball and toppings.

Adventurous addition: *A sprinkling of za'atar, a Middle Eastern spice blend, over the cheese before adding the spinach would be a flavor game-changer.*

Shaved Asparagus, Ricotta & Oven-Roasted Tomato Pizza

MAKES 2 (12- TO 14-INCH) PIZZAS OR 4 PERSONAL PIZZAS

Using a vegetable peeler to create thin ribbons of asparagus not only changes their shape but also their texture; paper-thin slices have a raw, refreshing quality, and visually, they add beautiful texture. Here they're paired with oven-roasted tomatoes for a fresh, light meal. When tomatoes aren't at their peak, a slow roast in the oven reduces their liquid and concentrates the flavor.

NUT-FREE

VEGETARIAN

PREP TIME: 15 minutes
COOK TIME: 1 hour
TOTAL TIME: 1 hour, 20 minutes

*For the oven-roasted tomatoes
(can be made up to 3 days in advance)*
4 tomatoes, cut into ¼-inch-thick slices
½ teaspoon salt
1 tablespoon extra-virgin olive oil
3 tablespoons balsamic vinegar, divided

For the pizza
Cornmeal or flour, for dusting
1 tablespoon extra-virgin olive oil,
    plus more for brushing
1 pound asparagus, shaved into long ribbons
    with a vegetable peeler
1 lemon wedge, for squeezing
¼ cup grated Parmesan cheese
¼ teaspoon fine sea salt
⅛ teaspoon freshly ground black pepper
Italian-Herbed Pizza Dough (page 37)
½ cup ricotta cheese

To make the oven-roasted tomatoes

1 Preheat the oven and pizza stone (if using) to 275°F. Line a baking sheet with foil.

2 Spread the tomatoes on the prepared baking sheet. Season with the salt, and drizzle with the olive oil and 1½ tablespoons of balsamic vinegar. Transfer to the oven and roast for 20 minutes, or until the tomatoes have collapsed. Drizzle the remaining 1½ tablespoons of balsamic vinegar over the tomatoes, and continue cooking for 20 minutes more, or until they are caramelized. Remove the baking sheet from the oven and transfer the tomatoes to a medium bowl.

LET'S
MAKE
PIZZA!

130

To make the pizza

1 Increase the oven temperature to 500°F. Dust a pizza peel with cornmeal (if using a pizza stone), or brush two baking sheets with olive oil.

2 In a medium bowl, toss together the asparagus, olive oil, a squeeze of lemon juice, and the Parmesan. Season with the salt and pepper and toss well.

3 Roll out one of the dough balls to the desired size, and place it on the pizza peel (if using a pizza stone) or on the prepared baking sheet.

4 Spoon half of the ricotta cheese in dollops all over the dough, spreading it evenly. Arrange half of the roasted tomatoes on top, followed by half of the asparagus mixture.

5 Transfer the pizza to the hot pizza stone or oven rack, and bake until the crust is golden and the cheese has melted, 5 to 7 minutes on the pizza stone or 7 to 10 minutes on the baking sheet.

6 Remove the pizza from the oven and transfer it to a cutting board. Let it rest for 5 minutes. Slice and serve.

7 Repeat from step 3 with the remaining dough ball and toppings.

A CLOSER LOOK: *Once the tomatoes are roasted, you can bring them to room temperature and refrigerate them in an airtight container for up to 3 days.*

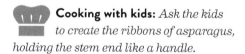 **Cooking with kids:** *Ask the kids to create the ribbons of asparagus, holding the stem end like a handle.*

Mushroom, Oven-Roasted Fennel & Taleggio Pizza

MAKES 2 (12- TO 14-INCH) PIZZAS OR 4 PERSONAL PIZZAS

Roasting fennel slowly and gently intensifies its anise flavor. While making pizza is a quick turnaround, oven roasting on low heat takes time. Make the fennel the night before for a much faster dinner.

PREP TIME: 10 minutes
COOK TIME: 1 hour, 25 minutes
TOTAL TIME: 1 hour, 40 minutes

For the oven-roasted fennel
5 fennel bulbs, stems and fronds removed, bulbs cut into ¼-inch-thick slices
3 tablespoons extra-virgin olive oil
¼ cup grated Parmesan cheese

For the mushrooms and pizza
Cornmeal or flour, for dusting
2 tablespoons extra-virgin olive oil, plus more for brushing
4 ounces cremini mushrooms, stems discarded, sliced
½ teaspoon dried thyme
Simply Amazing Pizza Dough (page 25) or Pro Dough (page 27)
½ pound Taleggio cheese, sliced

To make the oven-roasted fennel

Preheat the oven to 375°F. Spread the fennel on a baking sheet, toss with the olive oil to coat, then toss with the Parmesan. Bake for 45 minutes, until the fennel is tender.

To make the mushrooms and pizza

1 Preheat the oven and pizza stone (if using) to 500°F. Dust a pizza peel with cornmeal (if using a pizza stone), or brush two baking sheets with olive oil.

2 In a large skillet over medium-high heat, heat the olive oil. When it shimmers, add the mushrooms and thyme. Cook, undisturbed, for 3 to 4 minutes. Give the pan a shake and continue cooking until the mushrooms have released their moisture and are tender, 4 to 5 minutes more.

3 Roll out one of the dough balls to the desired size, and place it on the pizza peel (if using a pizza stone) or on the prepared baking sheet. Prick the dough several times with a fork, then transfer it to the hot stone or oven rack and bake for 3 to 4 minutes, until it just begins to turn color.

4 Remove the crust from the oven and top it with half of the mushrooms and fennel, followed by half of the Taleggio cheese.

5 Transfer the pizza to the hot pizza stone or oven rack, and bake until the crust is golden and the cheese is bubbling, 5 to 7 minutes on the pizza stone or 7 to 10 minutes on the baking sheet.

6 Remove the pizza from the oven and transfer it to a cutting board. Let it rest for 5 minutes. Slice and serve.

7 Repeat from step 3 with the remaining dough ball and toppings.

SUBSTITUTION TIP: *Taleggio is a soft sheep's milk cheese from Italy. Cut from squares, the cheese has a thin rind and is somewhat runny. With a strong aroma but mild taste, it melts beautifully. Fontina or Bel Paese can be used as a substitution.*

Seasonal Spotlight: Winter

Cold weather is all about coaxing the flavor out of winter produce. Oven-roasted root vegetables, burnished caramelized onions, and sautéed greens pair happily with richer cheeses and meatier flavors. Add color and a nutritional boost with oven-roasted squashes, broccoli, and Brussels sprouts. Winter pizzas are hearty affairs, so reach for Yukon gold potatoes, smoked hams, or bacon. And for vegans, sliced oven-roasted beets and sage make for a surprisingly satisfying "Beetza." Add a ray of sunshine by serving salads brightened by citrus or anchored by cooked vegetables.

Butternut Squash Pizza with Bacon & Blue Cheese

MAKES 2 (12- TO 14-INCH) PIZZAS OR 4 PERSONAL PIZZAS

PREP TIME: 10 minutes
COOK TIME: 1 hour
TOTAL TIME: 1 hour, 15 minutes

1 small (1-pound) butternut squash, peeled, seeded, and cut into small dice

3 tablespoons extra-virgin olive oil, plus more for brushing

¼ teaspoon salt, plus more for finishing

⅛ teaspoon freshly ground black pepper, plus more for finishing

3 fresh thyme sprigs, stemmed

4 slices center-cut bacon

Cornmeal or flour, for dusting

Simply Amazing Pizza Dough (page 25)

½ cup grated fontina cheese

¼ cup crumbled blue cheese

4 cups arugula

1 Preheat the oven and pizza stone to 400°F.

2 Spread the butternut squash on a foil-lined baking sheet and drizzle with the olive oil. Season with the salt, pepper, and thyme, and toss well. Bake until the squash is fork tender and golden, about 35 minutes, stirring and rotating the pan halfway through. Remove from the oven and cool briefly.

3 Meanwhile, in a sauté pan over medium heat, brown the bacon until crisp, 2 to 3 minutes per side. Transfer to a paper towel–lined plate and, when cool, roughly chop.

4 Raise the oven temperature to 500°F. Dust a pizza peel with cornmeal (if using a pizza stone), or brush two baking sheets with olive oil.

5 Roll out one of the dough balls to the desired size, and place it on the pizza peel or on the prepared baking sheet.

6 Spread half of the fontina and blue cheeses evenly over the dough. Top with half of the roasted butternut squash and half of the bacon.

7 Transfer the pizza to the hot pizza stone or oven rack, and bake until the crust is golden and the cheese is bubbly, 5 to 7 minutes on the pizza stone or 7 to 10 minutes on the baking sheet.

8 Remove the pizza from the oven and transfer it to a cutting board. Let it rest for 5 minutes, then top with half of the arugula. Slice and serve.

9 Repeat from step 5 with the remaining dough ball and toppings.

PREP TIP: *The butternut squash and bacon can be prepared the night before and refrigerated. This hearty pizza can be assembled and cooked in minutes.*

NUT-FREE

CALZONES

The calzone used to be pizza's forgotten cousin, sitting behind the counter at pizzerias, taking a back seat to the nonstop slices making their way from the oven into customers' hands.

Lately, however, there's been a resurgence of interest in calzones. Big and boldly flavored, these puffy, turnover-shaped hand pies are being redefined in chef-driven pizza restaurants around the country. In the home kitchen, they're a magnificent vehicle for building dinner with whatever you might have on hand. The guiding principal is cheese, marrying it all together.

The recipes in this chapter make two calzones each, but part of the fun is experimenting with size; make them smaller and they're snack food, bigger and they become a calzone statement. As with pizza, the entire assemblage can be as homemade or as store-bought as time and interest allow. Don't forget a small bowl of marinara sauce for dipping.

Classic Calzone

MAKES 2 CALZONES

These classic Margherita flavors tucked inside the pizza dough make it something like a sushi inside-out roll; change the order, and it's a whole different ball game. As with pizza, feel free to customize with pepperoni, red pepper flakes, or any of the dried spices.

▼
NUT-FREE

▼
VEGETARIAN

PREP TIME: 10 minutes
COOK TIME: 18 minutes
TOTAL TIME: 30 minutes

Extra-virgin olive oil, for greasing and brushing
¾ cup fresh ricotta cheese
¼ cup grated Parmesan cheese
¼ cup grated mozzarella cheese
2 tablespoons chopped fresh basil
¼ teaspoon salt
⅛ teaspoon pepper
All-purpose flour, for dusting
½ recipe (1 ball) Simply Amazing Pizza Dough (page 25) or Pro Dough (page 27), divided in half
½ cup New York–Style Pizza Sauce (page 40)

1 Preheat the oven to 500°F. Coat a baking sheet lightly with olive oil.

2 In a medium mixing bowl, combine the ricotta, Parmesan, and mozzarella cheeses, chopped basil, salt, and pepper.

3 On a lightly floured work surface, roll out the dough into 2 (6- to 8-inch) circles.

4 Spoon the sauce over each dough circle, leaving a half-inch border.

5 Spread half of the cheese mixture over half of each dough circle.

6 Moisten the edges with water, fold the dough over the filling, and pinch closed from end to end. Brush with olive oil and transfer to the prepared baking sheet.

7 Bake until the crust is golden and firm, 15 to 18 minutes, and serve.

COOKING TIP: *As with pizza, roll and stretch the dough thinly. If the dough shrinks back during the stretching, give it a 10-minute rest. The calzones can be cooked on a pizza stone, but I find it simpler (and safer!) to transport them on a baking sheet.*

Herbed Goat Cheese & Coppa Calzone

MAKES 2 CALZONES

A fragrantly herbaceous calzone, this one features the tang of goat cheese and the salty sweetness of coppa. The filling can be mixed a day before and refrigerated, ready to transform into a fast but sophisticated supper. If goat cheese isn't a favorite, substitute ricotta.

PREP TIME: 10 minutes
COOK TIME: 18 minutes
TOTAL TIME: 30 minutes

Extra-virgin olive oil, for greasing and brushing

4 slices sweet coppa, cut into thin strips

¾ cup fresh goat cheese, crumbled

6 ounces fresh mozzarella cheese, shredded

2 tablespoons finely chopped fresh chives

2 cups loosely packed chopped fresh flat-leaf parsley

2 tablespoons finely chopped fresh oregano

2 garlic cloves, minced

All-purpose flour, for dusting

½ recipe (1 ball) Simply Amazing Pizza Dough (page 25) or Pro Dough (page 27), divided in half

1 Preheat the oven to 500°F. Coat a baking sheet lightly with olive oil.

2 In a medium bowl, mix the coppa, goat cheese, mozzarella, chives, parsley, oregano, and garlic with a fork until well combined (add a drop or two of olive oil to soften the mixing process).

3 On a lightly floured work surface, roll out the dough into 2 (6- to 8-inch) circles.

4 Spoon the filling onto half of each circle, leaving a half-inch border. Moisten the edges with water, fold the dough over the filling, and pinch closed from end to end. Brush with olive oil and transfer to the prepared baking sheet.

5 Bake until the crust is golden brown and firm, about 15 to 18 minutes, and serve.

A CLOSER LOOK: *Sweet coppa is a dry-cured sausage made from pork shoulder. If unavailable, substitute your favorite salami, prosciutto, or American ham.*

Broccoli Rabe, Sausage & Ricotta Calzone

MAKES 2 CALZONES

Broccoli rabe and sausage is one of our family's favorite pasta, and the combination translates perfectly to calzone. Broccoli rabe has a pleasantly bitter taste, one that kids enjoy if blanched first, as indicated below. A good dose of red pepper flakes gives this combination the heat it needs to bring the flavors together.

PREP TIME: 10 minutes
COOK TIME: 30 minutes
TOTAL TIME: 40 minutes

2 tablespoons extra-virgin olive oil, plus more
　　for greasing and brushing
1 bunch broccoli rabe, stems trimmed, rinsed
2 garlic cloves, minced
¼ teaspoon red pepper flakes
3 sweet Italian sausages, removed from casings, sliced
All-purpose flour, for dusting
½ recipe (1 ball) Simply Amazing Pizza Dough
　　(page 25) or Pro Dough (page 27),
　　divided in half
1 cup fresh ricotta cheese
¼ cup grated mozzarella cheese
¼ cup grated Parmesan cheese
½ teaspoon salt
⅛ teaspoon freshly ground black pepper

1 Preheat the oven to 500°F. Coat a baking sheet lightly with olive oil.

2 Bring a large pot of salted water to a boil. Add the broccoli rabe, and blanch for 2 minutes. Using tongs, transfer the broccoli rabe to a large bowl of ice water. Drain, dry, and roughly chop.

3 In a medium sauté pan over medium heat, heat the olive oil. Add the chopped broccoli rabe, and quick sauté for 2 to 3 minutes to finish the cooking process. Add the garlic and red pepper flakes, cook 1 minute more, and transfer to a medium bowl.

4 Add the sausage meat to the pan and cook, stirring frequently with a fork, until no pink color remains, 5 to 6 minutes. Use a slotted spoon to transfer the meat to a bowl.

5 On a lightly floured work surface, roll out the dough into 2 (6- to 8-inch) circles.

6 Spoon the ricotta onto half of each circle, leaving a half-inch border. Top each with half of the mozzarella, Parmesan, salt, and pepper, then the sausage and broccoli rabe.

7 Moisten the edges with water, fold the dough over the filling, and pinch closed from end to end. Brush with olive oil and transfer to the prepared baking sheet.

8 Bake until the crust is golden brown and firm, about 15 to 17 minutes, and serve.

Keep it simple: *If your kids aren't ready for the spiciness of the red pepper flakes here, use half the amount or omit entirely and sprinkle on individual calzones as a topping after cooking.*

Chicken Pesto Calzone

MAKES 2 CALZONES

This calzone, with chicken and Basil Pesto, is part of the ongoing quest for tasty uses for boneless, skinless chicken breast. Pairing the chicken with Basil Pesto and ricotta is fresh, satisfying, and light (for a calzone, anyway). The recipe for chicken breasts described below, cooked in the oven under a sheet of parchment paper, is an ingenious method for keeping the breasts moist. Cook a few extra chicken breasts for a chicken salad made with mayonnaise flavored with Balsamic-Roasted Garlic (page 46)—lunchtime heaven. Or if you really want to save time, pick up a rotisserie chicken from the grocery store.

PREP TIME: 15 minutes
COOK TIME: 40 minutes
TOTAL TIME: 55 minutes

For the chicken

2 teaspoons extra-virgin olive oil, plus more for greasing

1 boneless, skinless chicken breast, pounded between two sheets of wax paper to a uniform thickness

½ teaspoon salt

⅛ teaspoon freshly ground black pepper

For the calzone

Extra-virgin olive oil, for greasing

All-purpose flour, for dusting

½ recipe (1 ball) Simply Amazing Pizza Dough (page 25) or Pro Dough (page 27), divided in half

2 slices prosciutto

1 cup fresh ricotta cheese

¼ cup grated mozzarella cheese

½ cup Basil Pesto (page 44)

⅛ teaspoon freshly ground black pepper

To make the chicken

1 Preheat the oven to 350°F. Line the bottom of a baking dish with parchment paper, and rub it and the sides of the dish with a little olive oil.

2 Season the chicken breast with the olive oil, salt, and pepper. Place the chicken breast in the baking dish, pressing it onto the oiled side of the parchment paper, and bake for 20 minutes.

3 Remove the chicken from the oven, let it cool slightly, then cut it against the grain into ½-inch slices.

To make the calzones

4 Increase the oven temperature to 500°F. Lightly grease a baking sheet with oil.

5 On a lightly floured work surface, roll out the dough into 2 (6- to 8-inch) circles.

6 Lay a prosciutto slice on one half of each of the circles, leaving a half-inch border. Top each with half of the chicken, ricotta, mozzarella, and Basil Pesto. Finish with pepper.

7 Moisten the edges with water, fold the dough over the filling, and pinch closed from end to end. Brush with olive oil and transfer to the prepared baking sheet.

8 Bake until the crust is golden brown and firm, about 15 to 18 minutes, and serve.

COOKING TIP: *In a time crunch, the time-saver bonanza of rotisserie chicken and outsourced pesto make this pizza a fast answer to the dinner question.*

Bacon, Egg & Sun-Dried Tomato Pesto Calzone

MAKES 2 CALZONES

A breakfast calzone, this is also perfect for those special nights when breakfast is what's for dinner. Sun-dried tomatoes processed into a pesto render their somewhat firm texture into a more appealing, spreadable condiment. Keep some on hand to serve with cheeses or on sandwiches.

PREP TIME: 10 minutes, plus 15 minutes to soak
COOK TIME: 25 minutes
TOTAL TIME: 50 minutes

For the sun-dried tomato pesto
4 ounces sun-dried tomatoes, coarsely chopped
1½ cups extra-virgin olive oil

For the calzone
Extra-virgin olive oil, for greasing
6 eggs
¼ teaspoon salt
⅛ teaspoon freshly ground black pepper
½ recipe (1 ball) Simply Amazing Pizza Dough (page 25) or Pro Dough (page 27), divided in half
2 ounces pancetta, diced, or center-cut bacon
½ cup grated Cheddar cheese
1 teaspoon chopped fresh oregano leaves

To make the sun-dried tomato pesto

In a medium bowl, soak the sun-dried tomatoes in the olive oil for 15 minutes. Transfer the mixture to a blender or food processor and purée to a smooth paste. The pesto can be stored, covered, in the refrigerator for up to 1 week. Stir before using.

To make the calzones

1 Preheat the oven to 500°F. Lightly grease a baking sheet with olive oil.

2 In a medium bowl, whisk the eggs with the salt and pepper.

3 In a medium sauté pan over medium heat, cook the pancetta until brown and crisp, about 6 minutes. Transfer to a paper towel–lined plate to cool, and discard the rendered fat.

4 Melt the butter in the pan. When it foams, add the whisked eggs. Softly scramble the eggs, moving them in the pan until they are no longer liquid, about 2 minutes. Turn off the heat.

5 On a lightly floured surface, roll out the dough into 2 (6- to 8-inch) circles.

6 Spoon a tablespoon of sun-dried tomato pesto on to each dough circle, and spread into a thin, even layer, leaving a half-inch border.

7 Top half of each dough circle with half of the scrambled eggs, pancetta, Cheddar, and oregano.

8 Moisten the edges with water, fold the dough over the filling, and pinch closed from end to end. Brush with olive oil and transfer to the prepared baking sheet.

9 Bake until the crust is golden brown and firm, 15 to 18 minutes, and serve.

Cooking with kids: *My experience with most kids has been that if they're tall enough to see into the pan, they're able to make scrambled eggs, a perfect first-time-at-the-stove task. They can break the eggs, whisk, season with salt and pepper, melt butter, and then pour the eggs into a sauté pan. With a wooden spoon, they can pull the outer eggs to the center as they firm up, repeating the motion until their softly scrambled eggs are complete.*

Caponata & Goat Cheese Calzone

MAKES 2 CALZONES

Caponata is eggplant relish, used as a condiment with cheese or as a topping for bruschetta. It is sold in jars but is easily and more deliciously made at home using the oven-roasting method described below, originally developed using a toaster oven.

PREP TIME: 15 minutes
COOK TIME: 1 hour, 10 minutes
TOTAL TIME: 1 hour 30 minutes

For the caponata

3 eggplants, about 10 inches each, peeled and cut into ½-inch dice
20 caper berries, stems removed, sliced thin
¼ teaspoon salt
⅛ teaspoon freshly ground black pepper
¼ teaspoon red pepper flakes
¼ cup extra-virgin olive oil
¼ cup balsamic vinegar
2 tablespoons honey
2 medium tomatoes, cored and diced
¼ cup pine nuts

For the calzone

All-purpose flour, for dusting
½ recipe (1 ball) Simply Amazing Pizza Dough (page 25) or Pro Dough (page 27), divided in half
¾ cup fresh ricotta cheese
1 cup caponata
¼ cup fresh goat cheese, crumbled
1 tablespoon chopped fresh parsley
Extra-virgin olive oil, for brushing

To make the caponata

1 Preheat the oven to 425°F. Line a baking sheet with foil.

2 Spread the eggplant and caper berries on the prepared baking sheet. Season with the salt, black pepper, and red pepper flakes.

3 In a small bowl, whisk together the olive oil, vinegar, and honey. Pour over the eggplant mixture and roast for 40 minutes, tossing the mixture every 10 minutes or so.

4 Add the tomatoes and roast for 10 minutes more. Toss with the pine nuts and cool to room temperature.

To make the calzones

1 Preheat the oven to 500°F.

2 On a lightly floured surface, roll out the dough into 2 (6- to 8-inch) circles.

3 Spoon the ricotta over half of each circle, leaving a half-inch boarder. Top each with half of the caponata, goat cheese, and parsley.

4 Moisten the edges with water, fold the dough over the filling, and pinch closed from end to end. Brush with olive oil and transfer to a lightly oiled baking sheet.

5 Bake until the crust is golden brown and firm, 15 to 18 minutes, and serve.

A CLOSER LOOK: *Caponata is Sicilian in origin; the boldly flavored mélange of eggplant and pine nuts is meant to have a sweet and sour balance that can be adjusted according to which side of the divide you fall on by adding either more vinegar or more honey. This version can be made up to 3 days in advance, kept covered in the refrigerator, and improves vastly over time. Use any leftover caponata in omelets or spooned over toast.*

Slow-Roasted Vegetable Whole-Wheat Calzone

MAKES 2 CALZONES

If calzones are the perfect vehicle for leftovers, sometimes "leftovers" are worth making fresh. Roasted vegetables, their sugars concentrated by the cooking process, are a convenient and crowd-pleasing way of serving vegetables. Easily made in advance, this is a healthier calzone and, with vegan cheese, a dairy-free option.

DAIRY-FREE

NUT-FREE

VEGETARIAN

PREP TIME: 15 minutes
COOK TIME: 55 minutes
TOTAL TIME: 1 hour, 10 minutes

3 tablespoons extra-virgin olive oil, plus more for greasing and brushing

2 cups diced butternut squash

1 red pepper, diced

1 yellow pepper, diced

1 cup diced carrots

1 teaspoon salt

½ teaspoon freshly ground black pepper

½ teaspoon dried oregano

All-purpose flour, for dusting

½ recipe (1 ball) Whole-Wheat Pizza Dough (page 29), divided in half

1 cup New York–Style Pizza Sauce (page 40)

½ cup shredded vegan mozzarella cheese

1 Preheat the oven to 450°F. Lightly grease a baking sheet with olive oil.

2 Spread the squash, red pepper, yellow pepper, and carrots on a separate baking sheet, drizzle with the olive oil, toss, and season with the salt, pepper, and oregano. Cook until the vegetables are fork tender and golden in color, about 35 minutes, turning them halfway through. Remove from the oven and cool briefly.

3 On a lightly floured surface, roll out the dough into 2 (6- to 8-inch) circles.

4 Spoon the sauce over the dough, spreading it thinly and evenly, leaving a half-inch border.

5 Top half of each circle with half of the roasted vegetables and vegan cheese.

6 Moisten the edges with water, fold the dough over the filling, and pinch closed from end to end. Brush with olive oil and transfer to the prepared baking sheet.

7 Bake until the crust is golden brown and firm, 15 to 18 minutes, and serve.

Adventurous addition: *Instead of a side of marinara sauce, the acidity of a salsa verde would be a welcome change. Use your favorite jarred version or make your own to serve as a dipping sauce.*

Kale, Chard & Caper Whole-Wheat Calzone

MAKES 2 CALZONES

There are babies who love olives. I've never had one, but I've seen them at parties, each finger topped with a black olive. This calzone, with deep, strong flavors that stand up to a whole-wheat dough, is for those kiddos. For everyone else, the olives and capers can be left out, with golden raisins added instead, depending on whether you're a sweet or salty type.

PREP TIME: 15 minutes
COOK TIME: 35 minutes
TOTAL TIME: 50 minutes

2 tablespoons extra-virgin olive oil,
    plus more for greasing and brushing
¼ cup walnuts
2 cups roughly chopped kale
2 cups roughly chopped Swiss chard
2 garlic cloves, minced
½ teaspoon red pepper flakes
1 tablespoon drained capers
½ cup Kalamata or Niçoise olives,
    pitted and roughly chopped
1 teaspoon balsamic vinegar
½ cup grated mozzarella cheese
½ cup ricotta cheese
All-purpose flour, for dusting
½ recipe (1 ball) Whole-Wheat Pizza Dough
    (page 29), divided in half

1 Preheat the oven to 450°F. Lightly grease a baking sheet with olive oil.

2 In a medium sauté pan over medium-low heat, toast the walnuts. Shake the pan frequently and heat the nuts until they are aromatic, about 3 minutes. Roughly chop and set aside.

3 In the same sauté pan over medium heat, heat the olive oil. When it shimmers, add the kale and chard. Cook for 5 minutes, tossing frequently with tongs. Add the garlic and red pepper flakes, and cook for 1 minute more.

4 Transfer the greens to a large sieve and press the liquid from them with the back of a spoon.

5 In a mixing bowl, combine the sautéed greens, capers, olives, and balsamic vinegar. Fold in the mozzarella and ricotta cheeses.

6 On a lightly floured surface, roll out the pizza dough into 2 (6- to 8-inch) circles.

7 Spoon the filling onto half of each circle, leaving a half-inch border. Brush the edges of the dough lightly with water, and fold over. Pinch the dough closed from end to end. Brush with olive oil and transfer to the prepared baking sheet.

8 Bake the calzone until golden brown and bubbly, 20 to 25 minutes, and serve.

Keep it simple: *Capers can be omitted here, but don't forget to compensate for their absence by sprinkling your calzones with salt before folding and sealing.*

Whipped Ricotta, Spinach & Sun-Dried Tomato Calzone

MAKES 2 CALZONES

The tried and true pairing of spinach and cheese is a natural for calzone. As always when using sautéed greens, pressing the moisture from the cooked leaves is key to preventing a soggy calzone.

PREP TIME: 10 minutes, plus 10 minutes to soak

COOK TIME: 30 minutes

TOTAL TIME: 50 minutes

5 tablespoons extra-virgin olive oil, divided, plus more for greasing and brushing

3 sun-dried tomatoes

⅔ cup ricotta cheese

⅓ cup feta cheese

2 tablespoons grated Parmesan cheese

1 egg yolk

Salt

Freshly ground black pepper

1 small yellow onion, finely diced (½ cup)

2 garlic cloves, minced

4 cups baby spinach, stems removed

All-purpose flour, for dusting

½ recipe (1 ball) Simply Amazing Pizza Dough (page 25) or Pro Dough (page 27), divided in half

1 Preheat the oven to 500°F. Lightly grease a baking sheet with olive oil.

2 In a small bowl, soak the sun-dried tomatoes in 3 tablespoons of olive oil for 10 minutes. Drain and chop.

3 In a large bowl, mix the ricotta, feta, Parmesan, and egg yolk until well combined. Season with salt and pepper. Set aside.

4 In a sauté pan over medium-high heat, heat the remaining 2 tablespoons of olive oil. When it shimmers, add the onion. Season with salt and pepper and cook, stirring frequently, until the onions are translucent, about 4 minutes. Add the garlic and cook until fragrant, about 1 minute more. Add the spinach to the pan and cook until the leaves have decreased in volume, about 3 minutes.

5 Transfer the spinach mixture to a sieve and, using the back of a spoon, press the moisture from the leaves. Transfer to a cutting board and roughly chop. Fold the chopped spinach and diced sun-dried tomatoes into the ricotta mixture.

6 On a lightly floured surface, roll out the pizza dough into 2 (6- to 8-inch) circles.

7 Spoon the spinach mixture onto half of each circle, leaving a half-inch border. Brush the edges with water and fold the dough over, pinching it closed from end to end. Transfer to the prepared baking sheet and brush lightly with olive oil.

8 Bake until the crust is firm and golden brown, 18 to 20 minutes, and serve.

Cooking with kids: *All mixing, measuring, and constructing of this calzone is kid friendly.*

Soppressata & Pepperoncini Calzone

MAKES 2 CALZONES

Soppressata and pepperoncini are two made-in-Italy products that can be found at most supermarkets. Soppressata, a dry Italian salami, pairs wonderfully with the hot pickled peppers of Tuscany, jarred and sold in full-service supermarkets.

PREP TIME: 10 minutes
COOK TIME: 20 minutes
TOTAL TIME: 30 minutes

Extra-virgin olive oil, for greasing and brushing
All-purpose flour, for dusting
½ recipe (1 ball) Simply Amazing Pizza Dough (page 25) or Pro Dough (page 27), divided in half
½ cup Classic Pizza Sauce
6 fresh basil leaves, torn
½ teaspoon dried oregano
1 garlic clove, minced
4 ounces fresh mozzarella cheese
3 slices soppressata, sliced into matchsticks
¾ cup ricotta cheese
1 pepperoncini, roughly chopped

1 Preheat the oven to 500°F. Lightly grease a baking sheet with olive oil.

2 On a lightly floured surface, roll out the pizza dough into 2 (6- to 8-inch) circles.

3 Spread the sauce over each dough circle in a thin, even layer, leaving a half-inch border. Top the sauce on each calzone with half of the basil leaves, oregano, and garlic, followed by half of the mozzarella and soppressata pieces on each. Spoon the ricotta over the other ingredients. Top each with a few pieces of chopped pepperoncini.

4 Brush the edges with water and fold the dough over, pinching it closed from end to end. Transfer to the prepared baking sheet and brush lightly with olive oil.

5 Bake in the oven for 18 to 20 minutes, until the dough is golden brown and firm, and serve.

Keep it simple: *If it's all too hot and spicy, skip the pepperoncini and use sweet oven-roasted red peppers (Peperonata, page 50) to mellow the flavor.*

Mushroom & Onion Fold-Over

MAKES 2 CALZONES

As a lifelong lover of quiche, onion tarts, or anything that features deeply burnished onions and the sweet tang of Gruyère and Swiss, I find this fold-over, a sort of open-face calzone, is one of my favorite uses for these ingredients.

▼

NUT-FREE

▼

VEGETARIAN

PREP TIME: 10 minutes
COOK TIME: 20 minutes
TOTAL TIME: 30 minutes

2 tablespoons extra-virgin olive oil,
    plus more for greasing and brushing
8 ounces button mushrooms, sliced and sautéed
½ cup Sweet Onion Jam (page 48)
½ teaspoon dried thyme
¼ teaspoon salt
⅛ freshly ground black pepper,
    plus more for finishing
All-purpose flour, for dusting
½ recipe (1 ball) Simply Amazing Pizza Dough
    (page 25), divided in half
½ cup grated Gruyère cheese
½ cup grated Swiss cheese

1 Preheat the oven to 500°F. Lightly grease a baking sheet with olive oil.

2 In a medium bowl, mix the sautéed mushrooms with the Sweet Onion Jam, thyme, salt, and pepper, stirring to combine.

3 On a lightly floured surface, roll out the pizza dough into 2 (6- to 8-inch) circles. Using half each of the grated Gruyère and Swiss cheeses, top each of the circles with a sprinkling, leaving a half-inch border, followed by the mushroom mixture. Top with the remaining Gruyère and Swiss cheeses, and season with pepper.

4 Brush the edges with water and fold the dough over, pinching it closed from end to end. Transfer to the prepared baking sheet, and brush lightly with olive oil.

5 Cook for 18 to 20 minutes, until the cheese has melted and the pizza dough is golden brown, and serve.

Keep it simple: *Since these fold-overs are a bit more free-form than standard calzones, the mushrooms can be easily omitted, transforming the final product into a more kid-friendly, but still sophisticated, take on grilled cheese.*

SALADS

Pizza night salads have to match the freewheeling, pitch-in spirit of the occasion, and they also have the additional responsibility of rounding out the meal.

Whether it's prewashed, organic mesclun or a straight-from-the-farm bunch of beets, there's the parental mandate to serve a vegetable or some green along with every meal. For pizza night, I aim for salads that relate to but don't repeat the flavors or ingredients on the pizza. So while I love a big wooden bowl of greens dressed with bacon, cheese, and croutons, pizza night salads should have a lighter hand and complete the meal. As quick and customizable as pizza itself, the salads served alongside should have an easy attitude. And, in a pinch, a handful of lightly dressed arugula tossed over a pepperoni pizza is a marvelous little dinner.

Home-Grown Garden Salad

SERVES 4

One of those great little salads that show how excellent ordinary ingredients can be when used at their summer peak, this salad is packed with crisp veggies. If most salads are built on the greens, this one flips the proportions, using the greens almost as a garnish and letting the vegetables have the stage.

PREP TIME: 15 minutes
COOK TIME: None
TOTAL TIME: 15 minutes

1 garlic clove, minced

3 tablespoons extra-virgin olive oil

2 teaspoons freshly squeezed lemon juice

2 teaspoons lemon zest

½ teaspoon dried oregano

3 cups mixed field greens

1 red pepper, cut into strips

1 yellow pepper, cut into strips

½ bunch radishes, sliced thin

1 zucchini, ends trimmed, cut lengthwise into thin ribbons

¼ teaspoon salt

⅛ teaspoon freshly ground black pepper

¼ pound Cacio de Roma cheese

1 In a salad bowl, whisk the garlic, olive oil, lemon juice, lemon zest, and oregano together.

2 Add the greens, red and yellow peppers, radishes, and zucchini ribbons. Season with the salt and pepper. Toss well, and serve the salad in small bowls topped with Cacio de Roma.

A CLOSER LOOK: *Cacio de Roma is a salty sheep's milk cheese with a pleasant, mild flavor. It's different without being too different. Ricotta salata would also work well with this salad.*

Oven-Roasted Beets with Spinach

SERVES 4

The quick road to veggie virtue, a salad of beets and spinach is a nutritious way to round out pizza night. If I happened to have some toasted pistachios or pumpkin seeds on hand, I would definitely toss them in.

▼

GLUTEN-FREE

▼

NUT-FREE

▼

VEGETARIAN

PREP TIME: 15 minutes
COOK TIME: 40 minutes
TOTAL TIME: 50 minutes

4 beets, washed, ends trimmed

2 tablespoons extra-virgin olive oil, plus more for rubbing

1 tablespoon freshly squeezed orange juice

1 tablespoon orange zest

1 teaspoon honey

2 teaspoons balsamic vinegar

3 cups baby spinach or mixed salad greens

¼ teaspoon salt

⅛ freshly ground black pepper

1 (4-ounce piece) pecorino romano cheese

1 Preheat the oven to 450°F.

2 Place the beets on squares of aluminum foil, rub with olive oil, and wrap in the foil. Transfer to a baking sheet and cook until easily pierced with the tip of a knife, about 40 minutes. Let cool completely, then rub the skins off the beets (wearing gloves to avoid staining, if preferred). Cut the beets into a medium dice.

3 In a salad bowl, whisk together the orange juice, orange zest, honey, balsamic, and olive oil. Add the diced beets.

4 Just before serving, add the spinach, salt, and pepper, and toss well. Use a vegetable peeler to shave curls of pecorino romano over each serving.

Fennel, Blood Orange, Black Olive & Shrimp Salad

SERVES 4

The addition of shrimp makes this quintessential winter salad of fennel and citrus feel a bit more special. Bold colors and bright flavors make this a wonderful pizza accompaniment. If you have Black Olive Tapenade (page 45) on hand, use it in place of the chopped olives.

GLUTEN-FREE

NUT-FREE

PREP TIME: 20 minutes
COOK TIME: 10 minutes
TOTAL TIME: 30 minutes

4 blood oranges
½ cup, plus 3 tablespoons extra-virgin olive oil
1 pound raw shrimp (about 20)
Salt
Freshly ground black pepper
2 fennel bulbs, outer layer removed, sliced thin
4 cups arugula, washed and spun dry
½ cup roughly chopped black olives

1 Using a large chef's knife, slice the top and bottom of the oranges off so that they stand flat on a cutting board. Slice the peel away from top to bottom in wide strips. When all of the peel has been removed, slice the segments away from the membrane, catching the juice in a small bowl. Set aside.

2 In a large sauté pan over medium-high heat, heat 3 tablespoons of olive oil. Season the shrimp with salt and pepper. When the oil shimmers, add the shrimp to the pan in 2 batches. Cook for 2 minutes per side, until opaque. Transfer to a plate. When cool enough to handle, peel the shrimp, split the backs with a paring knife, and devein.

3 In a salad bowl, use your hands to combine the sliced fennel and arugula. Season with salt and pepper, then add the orange segments and olives.

4 Whisk the remaining ½ cup of olive oil into the bowl of reserved blood orange juice, and dress the salad.

5 Toss the cooked shrimp in the bowl used to mix the olive oil and orange juice, moistening them.

6 Divide the salad among 4 bowls, topping each with a handful of the shrimp. Season with salt and pepper, and serve.

COOKING TIP: *Sauté the shrimp up to 2 hours in advance, and keep at room temperature. Peel just before using, or to save time, purchase cooked and cleaned shrimp.*

Shaved Brussels Sprout Salad

SERVES 4

GLUTEN-FREE

VEGETARIAN

Our neighborhood restaurant, Jonathan Waxman's Barbuto, is the only place my children routinely ask for a second order of salad. Needless to say, I've recreated all of them in my home kitchen. This one is utterly simple and beyond delicious with pizza. A Japanese Benriner mandoline brings it all together in minutes.

PREP TIME: 10 minutes
COOK TIME: 4 minutes
TOTAL TIME: 15 minutes

1 cup hazelnuts or walnuts
1½ pounds Brussels sprouts
¼ cup extra-virgin olive oil
Juice of 1 lemon (about 4 tablespoons)
Sea salt
Freshly ground black pepper
3 tablespoons finely grated pecorino romano cheese

1 In a medium sauté pan over medium-low heat, toast the walnuts. Shake the pan frequently and heat the nuts until they are aromatic, about 4 minutes. Remove from the heat and roughly chop. Set aside.

2 Slice each Brussels sprout using a mandoline held over a salad bowl. Hold by the stem end and cut into thin slices. Add the walnuts.

3 In a small bowl, whisk to combine the olive oil and lemon juice. Season with salt and pepper. Dress the salad just before serving, tossing to distribute the dressing. Break the sprout slices into shreds, then sprinkle on the cheese.

Cooking with kids: *Knowing how to make a simple salad dressing of olive oil and lemon is a good life skill. Ask the kids to toss the salad with their clean hands for even coverage. Just keep them away from the mandoline.*

The Hampton Classic

SERVES 4 TO 6

This salad is so named because it's seen on practically every table on Long Island's East End, each one altered slightly based on the preferences of its maker. Tossed or composed, spicy or sweet, they all begin with the surprisingly delicious combination of watermelon and feta. This summertime favorite is loved by all for its simplicity, good looks, and undeniably satisfying blend of flavors. It's a natural fit for any grilled pizza party.

PREP TIME: 10 minutes
COOK TIME: 2 minutes
TOTAL TIME: 12 minutes

½ cup shelled pistachios
2 tablespoons balsamic vinegar
2 tablespoons extra-virgin olive oil
3 cups arugula
1 cup fresh mint leaves, roughly chopped
4 cups diced, seedless watermelon (about 1½-inch dice)
1½ cups crumbled feta
¼ teaspoon salt
¼ teaspoon freshly ground black pepper

1 In a small sauté pan over medium heat, swirl the nuts until they are aromatic, about 2 minutes. Remove from the heat and roughly chop.

2 In a small bowl, whisk the vinegar and olive oil together.

3 On a deep platter, use your hands to combine the arugula, mint, and watermelon. Add the feta and pistachios.

4 Drizzle the oil and vinegar over the salad and season with the salt and pepper just before serving.

COOKING TIP: *Feta is a salty cheese and will draw the liquid from the watermelon. If making this salad ahead, reserve the watermelon, adding it just before dressing and serving.*

Jersey Corn & Tomato Salad

SERVES 4

A natural grilled pizza partner, this one is a childhood favorite that featured the peerless beefsteak tomatoes grown in New Jersey. As they're hard to find (even in my home state), I use multicolored cherry tomatoes; their jewel-like appearance brings a little natural glamour to the bowl. If you can find bicolored corn, grab it. The corn can be grilled hours in advance and kept at room temperature.

PREP TIME: 15 minutes
COOK TIME: 10 minutes
TOTAL TIME: 25 minutes

1 small red onion, sliced thin

8 ears sweet summer corn, shucked

3 tablespoons extra-virgin olive oil, plus more for rubbing

1 pint multicolored cherry tomatoes

1 cup torn fresh basil leaves

2 tablespoons chopped fresh oregano

2 tablespoons red wine vinegar

¼ teaspoon salt, plus extra for the tomatoes

⅛ teaspoon freshly ground black pepper

1 Preheat the grill or a grill pan on the stove to high heat.

2 In a small bowl of water, soak the onion slices.

3 Rub each ear of corn with a little olive oil. On the grill or grill pan over high heat, cook the corn, about 3 to 4 minutes per side, letting the corn take some char from the grill. Let cool.

4 Meanwhile, strain the onion slices and press between paper towels to dry.

5 In a salad bowl, halve the cherry tomatoes. Lightly salt them to draw a bit of their liquid out.

6 Cut the kernels from the cobs and add to the tomatoes. Toss the salad with the basil leaves and oregano.

7 In a small bowl, whisk to combine the olive oil, vinegar, salt, and pepper. Dress the salad just before serving.

COOKING TIP: *If you're not grilling the corn, cut the kernels from the cob and sauté them in 1½ tablespoons of olive oil for 3 to 5 minutes, depending on the freshness and sweetness of the corn (fresh, tender summer corn will require less cooking time). Season with ¼ teaspoon of salt.*

Green Beans with Shallots

SERVES 4

This simple side can be served hot or at room temperature, making it extremely useful in rounding out pizza night with a vegetable side dish. Top with a sprinkling of any herb you have on hand.

GLUTEN-FREE

NUT-FREE

VEGAN

PREP TIME: 10 minutes
COOK TIME: 8 minutes
TOTAL TIME: 18 minutes

1 pound green beans, stem ends trimmed

3 tablespoons extra-virgin olive oil

2 shallots, peeled and sliced

Salt

Freshly ground black pepper

3 tablespoons white wine vinegar

2 teaspoons Dijon mustard

1 Bring a large pot of salted water to a boil. Blanch the beans until just tender, about 4 minutes. Transfer to a bowl of ice water, then drain.

2 In a large sauté pan, heat the olive oil over medium heat. When it shimmers, add the shallots and cook for 4 minutes, until soft and fragrant. Add the green beans and toss to combine. Season with salt and pepper, and transfer to a serving bowl.

3 Add the white wine vinegar and mustard to the still-warm pan, and swirl into the olive oil. Season with salt and pepper, pour over the beans, and serve.

 Cooking with kids: *Trimming the stem end from green beans is one of those somewhat tedious jobs that promote conversation. Sit down together for a chat. The kids can snap them off or use a small paring knife.*

Caesar Salad with Candied Walnuts

SERVES 4

Candied walnuts and a richly layered Caesar dressing bring out the best in crisp romaine leaves. This little twist on the classic Caesar adds a surprising sweetness to the picture that seems like it should have been there all along.

Balsamic-Roasted Garlic (page 46) has countless uses, one of the best being an ingredient in salad dressings. If you don't have Balsamic-Roasted Garlic on hand, drizzle a head of garlic (the top of it sliced off, exposing the cloves) with olive oil, wrap in foil, and roast in a 400°F oven for 40 minutes.

PREP TIME: 15 minutes
COOK TIME: 10 minutes
TOTAL TIME: 25 minutes

For the dressing
4 cloves Balsamic-Roasted Garlic (page 46)
2 teaspoons Dijon mustard
½ tablespoon white wine vinegar
2 tablespoons sherry vinegar
1 egg yolk
4 anchovy fillets
Juice of half a lemon
¾ cup extra-virgin olive oil

For the candied walnuts
2 egg whites
3 tablespoons dark brown sugar
2 tablespoons honey
2 cups walnut halves

For the salad
2 heads romaine lettuce, ends trimmed, leaves left whole
½ cup grated pecorino romano cheese

To make the dressing

In a blender, combine the Balsamic-Roasted Garlic, mustard, white wine and sherry vinegars, egg yolk, anchovies, and lemon juice. With the blender running, add the olive oil in a slow, steady stream until the mixture is smooth. Transfer to a jar, and refrigerate for up to a week.

To make the candied walnuts

1 Preheat the oven to 300°F.

2 In a small bowl, whisk the egg whites until thickened, about 3 minutes. Whisk in the brown sugar and honey. Add the walnuts and stir to coat. Use a slotted spoon to transfer the nuts to a parchment-lined baking tray. Bake for 10 minutes. Let cool completely. The nuts can be stored in an airtight container for up to 2 weeks.

To make the salad

In a large salad bowl, toss the dressing, romaine leaves, and cheese. Serve immediately, topping each salad serving with a few candied walnuts.

PREP TIP: *The Balsamic-Roasted Garlic can be made up to 3 days in advance.*

Kale Salad with Anchovy Vinaigrette

SERVES 4

With no egg yolk, this Caesar-inspired salad has a lighter quality than the traditional. As always with raw kale, massaging the dressing into the leaves goes a long way toward softening the leaves, and, as kitchen tasks go, it's delightfully relaxing. I find there are things that kids are happy to eat if they haven't seen what goes into it; anchovies are one of those things. I slip them in on the down low. If it's summer pizza grilling season, grilled squid is a great addition to this—in which case I call it the Squ-easer.

GLUTEN-FREE

NUT-FREE

PREP TIME: 10 minutes
COOK TIME: None
TOTAL TIME: 10 minutes

2 anchovy fillets

1 garlic clove, smashed

12 fresh basil leaves, roughly chopped

2 teaspoons Dijon mustard

Juice of 1 lemon

¾ cup extra-virgin olive oil

4 cups ribbed, chopped kale

¼ teaspoon salt

⅛ teaspoon freshly ground black pepper

½ cup grated pecorino romano cheese

1 In a blender, pulse to combine the anchovies, garlic, basil leaves, mustard, and lemon juice.

2 With the blender running, add the olive oil in a slow, steady stream.

3 In a salad bowl, dress the kale leaves with the dressing. Rub the dressing into the kale leaves, coating each leaf.

4 Season the salad with the salt and pepper, sprinkle with the cheese, and serve.

Cooking with kids: *Many salad gurus are convinced that massaging kale relaxes the leaves and tenderizes them. I'm not sure if that's true or not, but it is an ideal way to achieve a well-dressed green. Ask the kids to give the greens a rubdown, with clean hands.*

Celery & Chickpea Salad

SERVES 4

When you have no salad greens, this is the salad; made from ingredients that are available even in snowy ski town supermarkets, this deliciously satisfying salad brings together canned chickpeas and celery, which, lest we forget, has an elegant flavor and crisp crunch—always appreciated with pizza. An added advantage: It tastes best if made in advance, giving the lemon flavor a chance to mingle. Add sliced raw mushrooms instead of chickpeas as a variation. Add the greens from the celery. Use all of it to enhance the flavor.

GLUTEN-FREE

▼

VEGAN

PREP TIME: 10 minutes
COOK TIME: None
TOTAL TIME: 10 minutes

1 garlic clove, roughly chopped
3 tablespoons extra-virgin olive oil
Juice of 1 lemon
⅛ teaspoon ground cumin
¼ teaspoon salt
⅛ teaspoon freshly ground black pepper
5 celery stalks, sliced thin on a mandoline (3 cups)
1 (15.5-ounce) can chickpeas, rinsed and drained
½ cup flat-leaf parsley leaves, roughly chopped
Leafy greens from the celery, roughly chopped

1 In a salad bowl, crush the garlic with a pestle or meat tenderizer. Add the olive oil, lemon juice, cumin, salt, and pepper, and whisk to combine.

2 Add the celery, chickpeas, parsley, and celery greens. Toss thoroughly, and serve.

 Adventurous addition: *Add flaked tuna, grilled shrimp, or octopus to evoke a sunny day on the Mediterranean—even in the depths of winter.*

SALADS

169

Beet, Pistachio & Watercress Salad

SERVES 4

This plated salad takes minutes to assemble after roasting the beets, which can be done well in advance. Watercress, as part of the ongoing rotation of salad greens, is a good source of antioxidants and vitamins. With roasted beets, this salad is healthy, pretty, and delicious. Ricotta salata, an almost crumbly sheep's milk cheese, adds a salty dimension. Feta would be a good substitute.

PREP TIME: 10 minutes
COOK TIME: 1 hour
TOTAL TIME: 1 hour, 10 minutes

For the beets
4 beets
3 tablespoons extra-virgin olive oil
½ teaspoon salt
¼ teaspoon freshly ground black pepper

For the dressing and the salad
2 tablespoons red wine vinegar
¼ cup extra-virgin olive oil
1 teaspoon ground cumin
1 teaspoon honey
1 teaspoon Dijon mustard
2 teaspoons sparkling water
¼ teaspoon salt
Pinch freshly ground black pepper
2 fresh thyme sprigs, stemmed
4 cups watercress, rinsed and spun dry
½ cup roughly chopped pistachio nuts
2 ounces ricotta salata cheese, sliced

To make the beets

1 Preheat the oven to 450°F.

2 Rinse and dry the beets, trimming the stem ends. Place each beet on a square of aluminum foil, drizzle with the olive oil, and season with the salt and pepper. Wrap the beets in their foil, place on a baking sheet, and bake until easily pierced with the tip of a knife, about 1 hour.

To make the dressing and the salad

1 Meanwhile, in a jar, combine the vinegar, olive oil, cumin, honey, mustard, and sparkling water. Shake before using.

2 Remove the beets from the foil and, when ready to use, rub the skins from the beets. Cut into a medium-size dice.

3 In a mixing bowl, spoon 2 tablespoons of dressing over the beets and lightly toss. Season with the salt, pepper, and thyme.

4 When ready to serve, in a salad bowl, toss the watercress with the dressing. Divide the watercress among 4 serving bowls and top with the diced roasted beets. Sprinkle each with pistachios and a slice of ricotta salata.

COOKING TIP: *Hands that have cut roasted beets are tinted beet red for a day or two afterward. Wear latex kitchen gloves to prevent this, or wash your hands with the cut side of a potato to remove most of the stain.*

Roasted Cauliflower with Marcona Almonds & Parsley

SERVES 4

This simple but distinctive salad treats parsley as a salad green, giving a lightness to the deep, roasted flavor of cauliflower. Hailing from Spain, Marcona almonds have a more full-bodied flavor then regular almonds, adding an almost meaty quality. The nuts are expensive and can burn quickly in the oven, so keep an eye on them. Pistachios would make a good substitute. When cutting the cauliflower florets from the head, keep the stems on the short side, on scale with the parsley leaves. This salad is made in heavy rotation in my kitchen, with pizza or with the addition of ½ cup of clothbound Cheddar when served with other dishes that don't already contain cheese.

PREP TIME: 10 minutes
COOK TIME: 25 minutes
TOTAL TIME: 35 minutes

½ cup Marcona almonds

1 head cauliflower, cut into florets

¼ cup plus 3 tablespoons extra-virgin olive oil, divided

½ teaspoon salt

¼ teaspoon freshly ground black pepper

1 cup flat-leaf parsley leaves (tightly packed)

1½ tablespoons balsamic vinegar

2 teaspoons freshly squeezed lemon juice

1 Preheat the oven to 200°F.

2 Place the nuts on a baking sheet, and lightly toast for 3 to 4 minutes, until they are aromatic. Let cool and roughly chop.

3 Raise the oven temperature to 450°F.

4 Spread the cauliflower florets on a foil-lined baking sheet. Drizzle 3 tablespoons of olive oil over them and toss to coat. Season with the salt and pepper.

5 Roast the cauliflower until tender and golden, about 20 minutes, tossing the florets twice during the cooking process. Let cool to room temperature.

6 In a salad bowl, toss to combine the cauliflower, chopped nuts, and parsley leaves.

7 In a small bowl, whisk the remaining ¼ cup of olive oil, balsamic vinegar, and lemon juice together. Dress the salad just before serving.

COOKING TIP: *The nuts can be toasted up to 1 week in advance, and the cauliflower can be roasted the night before and refrigerated. Let the cauliflower come to room temperature before using.*

THE DIRTY DOZEN & THE CLEAN FIFTEEN

A nonprofit and environmental watchdog organization called Environmental Working Group (EWG) looks at data supplied by the US Department of Agriculture (USDA) and the Food and Drug Administration (FDA) about pesticide residues and compiles a list each year of the best and worst pesticide loads found in commercial crops. You can refer to the Dirty Dozen list to know which fruits and vegetables you should always buy organic. The Clean Fifteen list lets you know which produce is considered safe enough when grown conventionally to allow you to skip the organics. This does not mean that the Clean Fifteen produce is pesticide-free, though, so wash these fruits and vegetables thoroughly. These lists change every year, so make sure you look up the most recent before you fill your shopping cart. You'll find the most recent lists as well as a guide to pesticides in produce at www.EWG.org/FoodNews.

DIRTY DOZEN

Apples
Celery
Cherry tomatoes
Cucumbers
Grapes
Nectarines
Peaches
Potatoes
Snap peas
Spinach
Strawberries
Sweet bell peppers

In addition to the Dirty Dozen, the EWG added two foods contaminated with highly toxic organo-phosphate insecticides:

Hot peppers
Kale/Collard greens

CLEAN FIFTEEN

Asparagus
Avocados
Cabbage
Cantaloupe
Cauliflower
Eggplant
Grapefruit
Kiwis
Mangos
Onions
Papayas
Pineapples
Sweet corn
Sweet peas (frozen)
Sweet potatoes

MEASUREMENT CONVERSIONS

VOLUME EQUIVALENTS (LIQUID)

US STANDARD	US STANDARD (OUNCES)	METRIC (APPROXIMATE)
2 tablespoons	1 fl. oz.	30 mL
¼ cup	2 fl. oz.	60 mL
½ cup	4 fl. oz.	120 mL
1 cup	8 fl. oz.	240 mL
1½ cups	12 fl. oz.	355 mL
2 cups or 1 pint	16 fl. oz.	475 mL
4 cups or 1 quart	32 fl. oz.	1 L
1 gallon	128 fl. oz.	4 L

OVEN TEMPERATURES

FAHRENHEIT	CELSIUS (APPROXIMATE)
250°F	120°C
300°F	150°C
325°F	165°C
350°F	180°C
375°F	190°C
400°F	200°C
425°F	220°C
450°F	230°C

VOLUME EQUIVALENTS (DRY)

US STANDARD	METRIC (APPROXIMATE)
⅛ teaspoon	0.5 mL
¼ teaspoon	1 mL
½ teaspoon	2 mL
¾ teaspoon	4 mL
1 teaspoon	5 mL
1 tablespoon	15 mL
¼ cup	59 mL
⅓ cup	79 mL
½ cup	118 mL
⅔ cup	156 mL
¾ cup	177 mL
1 cup	235 mL
2 cups or 1 pint	475 mL
3 cups	700 mL
4 cups or 1 quart	1 L

WEIGHT EQUIVALENTS

US STANDARD	METRIC (APPROXIMATE)
½ ounce	15 g
1 ounce	30 g
2 ounces	60 g
4 ounces	115 g
8 ounces	225 g
12 ounces	340 g
16 ounces or 1 pound	455 g

REFERENCES

BBC News. "Pizza Sets New Delivery Record." May 22, 2001. news.bbc.co.uk /2/hi/americas/1345139.stm.

Kuban, Adam. "What is VPN Pizza?" Seriouseats.com. June 24, 2011. slice.seriouseats.com/archives/2011/06/what-is-vpn-pizza.html.

Levine, Ed. *Pizza: A Slice of Heaven*. Rizzoli Universe Promotional Books, April 20, 2010.

Lopez-Alt, Kenji. "Jim Lahey's No Knead Pizza Dough." March 20, 2012. seriouseats.com/recipes/2012/03/jim-laheys-no-knead-pizza-dough -recipe.html

Moses, Paul. *An Unlikely Union: The Love-Hate Story of New York's Irish and Italians*. NYC: NYU Press, July 3, 2015.

NASA. "3D Printing: Food in Space." May 23, 2013. www.nasa.gov /directorates/spacetech/home/feature_3d_food_prt.htm.

Turner, Geoff. "A Canadian Invented the Hawaiian Pizza." *The Toronto Sun*. July 14, 2010. http://www.torontosun.com/news/canada/2010/07/14 /14706791.html.

Zaino, Caitlin. "The Deep-Rooted History of Chicago's Deep-Dish Pizza." BBC Travel. October 25, 2013. www.bbc.com/travel/story/20131023-the -deep-rooted-history-of-chicagos-deep-dish-pizza.

INDEX